MORE Hampshire MURDERS

NICOLA SLY

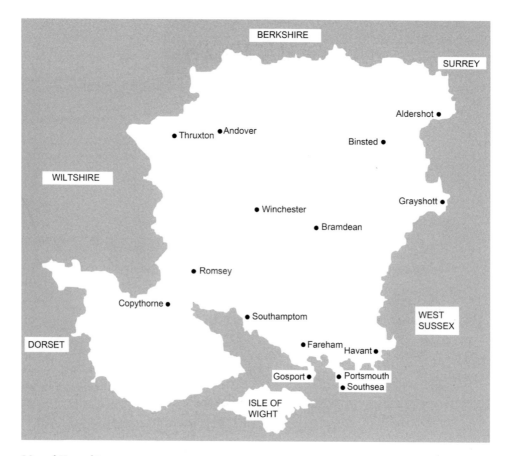

Map of Hampshire.

First published 2010

The History Press
The Mill, Brimscombe Port
Stroud, Gloucestershire, GL5 2QG
www.thehistorypress.co.uk

British Library Cataloguing in Publication Data.
A catalogue record for this book is available from the British Library.

ISBN 978 0 7524 5495 5

Typesetting and origination by The History Press
Printed in Great Britain
Manufacturing managed by Jellyfish Print Solutions Ltd

CONTENTS

Introduction & Acknowledgements   5

1.   'An officer and a gentleman on every occasion'
     Off Portsmouth, 1802   7

2.   'Who or what is it the bastard wants?'
     Fareham, 1827   11

3.   'What the devil have you been up to?'
     Portsmouth, 1830   15

4.   'Now I'll tell you the truth'
     Bramdean, near Alresford, 1836   20

5.   'I will shoot him like a partridge'
     Gosport, 1845   24

6.   'I have done for your fancy old bastard after all'
     Romsey, 1851   29

7.   'If I am not greatly mistaken, it was a man with plenty
     of money and a very bad wife'
     Andover, 1858   35

8.   'If you forget to be a son, I shall forget to be a father'
     Gosport, 1860   44

9.   'What harm have I ever done you?'
     Aldershot, 1861   48

10. 'I think he is cracked, Fred'
     Shirley, near Southampton, 1864   51

11. 'Oh, mother, my poor mother'
     Portsea, 1865   58

12. 'I know what I have done and I am not sorry for it'
     Aldershot, 1869   62

13. 'I did it because he should not have her'
     Newtown, Aldershot, 1888   67

14. 'I am watched all over the place like a clock watch'
    Portsmouth, 1888   71

15. 'There's a man killing a boy round yonder!'
    Havant, 1888   76

16. 'I am the victim of a terrible infatuation'
    Stamshaw, Portsmouth, 1891   85

17. 'Hurry along or we shall be late home'
    Southsea, 1893   92

18. 'That will be the last cup of tea you shall fling at me'
    Binsted, 1894   100

19. 'Promise you'll be good to her'
    Copnor, 1896   104

20. 'If you ever leave me, you will go a limb short'
    Southampton, 1896   111

21. 'Poor baby is so ill'
    Rowney, 1898   116

22. 'Vengeance is mine, sayeth the Lord. I will repay'
    Grayshott, 1901   120

23. 'Yes, it's a funny job'
    Gosport, 1902   125

24. 'They will murder some of us up there some day'
    Aldershot, 1903   130

25. 'A good son to a bad mother'
    Pollard's Moor, Copythorne, 1913   136

26. 'I will kill or be killed'
    Thruxton Down, near Andover, 1920   139

27. 'I will make sure he is finished and then finish myself'
    Southampton, 1931   145

28. 'There just has to be an end to it'
    Southampton, 1932   149

    Bibliography & References   152
    Index   153

INTRODUCTION & ACKNOWLEDGEMENTS

The most difficult part of writing my book *Hampshire Murders* (2009) was deciding which of the county's fascinating historical murders to leave out of the collection. It quickly became apparent that Hampshire merited a second compilation of cases.

These include the murders of William Harmsworth in 1827, Caroline Colborne in 1864, and Emily Chapman in 1901 – all due to jealousy – and the last ever fatal duel in England, which took place in 1845 near Gosport. The dreadful murder of schoolboy Percy Knight Searle in 1888 remains unsolved – did the infamous 'Jack the Ripper' pay a visit to Havant? And what was the motive for the brutal murder of five-year-old Emma Downton in Southsea in 1901 by the most unlikely of killers?

As always, there are numerous people to be acknowledged and thanked for their help in compiling this book. The cases were mainly drawn from national and local newspapers which, along with any books consulted, are listed in detail in the bibliography. The Hampshire Record Office were tremendously helpful with my research. Every effort has been made to clear copyright, however my apologies to anyone I may have missed; I can assure you it was not deliberate but an oversight on my part.

On a more personal level, my long-suffering husband, Richard, performed his usual miracles, uncomplainingly proofreading every word of the book and offering invaluable suggestions on how each chapter could be improved. And, last, but not least, my thanks go to my editors at The History Press, Matilda Richards, Beth Amphlett and Jenny Briancourt, for their help and encouragement.

Nicola Sly, 2010

A Hampshire police constable from the early 1920s. (Author's collection)

1

'AN OFFICER AND A GENTLEMAN ON EVERY OCCASION'

Off Portsmouth, 1802

On 6 January 1802, HMS *Resistance* was preparing to sail to the West Indies and Lieutenant Thomas Henry Lutwidge was sent ashore with a party of sailors to buy provisions for the voyage.

The task took much longer than expected, mainly because the sailors seized the opportunity of being ashore to drink themselves almost senseless. By the time Lieutenant Lutwidge had rounded up his errant crew – one of whom had actually deserted – it was almost half-past seven in the evening. The tide was about to turn and the wind was against them and it looked doubtful that they would be able to return to the ship that night. Yet even with the odds against them, and several of the crew roaring drunk, Lutwidge decided to risk the four-mile trip

One of the sailors, named only as J. Fagan, had been staggering about on the quay. On boarding the launch, he took possession of an oar, but in his state of inebriation, he was unable to row properly and his ineptitude was impeding the oar strokes of the remaining sailors. With time of the essence, Lutwidge ordered another sailor to take over Fagan's oar, but when the sailor approached him and passed on the order, Fagan refused to relinquish it, insisting that he could manage.

Lutwidge again ordered the sailor to take Fagan's oar, this time shouting to Fagan, commanding him to hand it over. Once again, Fagan refused, stating that he was quite capable of rowing.

Exasperated, Lutwidge seized the tiller of the launch on which he had been leaning and struck the sailor he had ordered to relieve Fagan on the arm. He then made his way down the boat, tiller in hand, and struck Fagan twice, once on the arm and once on the head. Fagan slumped to the bottom of the boat and the oar was finally taken from him. The party successfully reached their ship, where Fagan was hoisted aboard and put to bed under the care of his messmates.

The next morning, Mr Neale, the surgeon's mate of the *Resistance* was called to examine Fagan who was still unresponsive. Neale found that Fagan was dead but when he remonstrated with the sailors sharing Fagan's quarters for not calling him sooner, he was told that they had assumed that he was only drunk and had therefore been reluctant to call for any assistance. Mr Neale performed a cursory examination of the body and decided that Fagan had died through suffocation or apoplexy brought about by intoxication. The body was removed to the dead cell on the ship and Mr Stevenson, the surgeon from Haslar Naval Hospital, was called to examine the body. Stevenson concurred with Neale's opinion on the cause of death.

The captain of the *Resistance*, Captain Digby, questioned the crew to see if they had any complaints, promising to give them a fair hearing if they did. No complaint was made, but Digby was approached by one crewmember – Lieutenant Lutwidge. Lutwidge told the captain that he had hit Fagan and that he believed that the blow to Fagan's head was the most probable cause of his death.

Mr Neale and Mr Stevenson were called back to re-examine the body but neither man could find any evidence of an injury to Fagan's head. Both of the medical men continued to insist that Fagan had died as a direct result of his drunkenness but, in order to make absolutely certain, Mr Stevenson eventually asked the ship's barber to shave the dead man's head. At first glance, Mr Stevenson was still unable to locate any signs of a head injury but, on carefully feeling the shaved skull, he eventually detected what he described as 'a small tumour', less than the size of his fingertip, which yielded when he pressed it. Watched by Lieutenant Lutwidge among others, the surgeon took a scalpel and carefully removed a section of Fagan's scalp, revealing a small fracture of the skull, which had evidently caused fragments of bone to press upon Fagan's brain.

Mr Stevenson described the external appearance of the wound as 'trifling' and stated that he was unable to tell whether it had occurred as the result of a fall or a blow. Neither was he able to reliably estimate the degree of force that would have been necessary to cause the depressed fracture.

The entrance to the Royal Naval Hospital, Haslar, 1908. (Author's collection)

An inquest was opened at Gosport and, with clear evidence of a head injury, coupled with Lutwidge's admission that he had hit Fagan over the head the coroner's jury had little hesitation in returning a verdict of wilful murder against him. His trial took place at Winchester in March 1802, before Mr Justice Le Blanc.

The first witness called was a sailor who, to the consternation of the court, appeared on the witness stand drunk, even though it was only eight o'clock in the morning! Reporting the trial on 17 March, *The Times* commented 'Of this man, we shall only say, that his demeanour to the judge taught us not to expect a very ready obedience to his superiors when in this condition.'

However, despite his obvious inebriation on the witness stand, the sailor's evidence concurred with that of the other witnesses, particularly sailor Henry Warren who had been one of the landing party charged with buying supplies. Warren recounted the events of the 6 January, adding that none of the party had believed Fagan to be hurt, or they would have called the surgeons to attend to him.

After Mr Neale and Mr Stevenson had testified, there followed a stream of witnesses both from the *Resistance* and from Lutwidge's previous ship the *Endymion,* who testified to Lutwidge's good character. The lieutenant was variously described as 'mild and good tempered', 'humane and kind' and 'an officer and a gentleman on every occasion'. Two witnesses even went as far as to state that Lutwidge was 'universally beloved by every man and boy on the ship'.

In fact, all who testified portrayed Lieutenant Lutwidge almost as a saint, eventually forcing the judge to intervene and put a halt to the lengthy procession of people who were ready and waiting to speak on behalf of the accused. Asking the jury if they were satisfied with the evidence they had heard so far with regard to the previous good character of the prisoner and receiving assurances that they were, he politely suggested to the defence counsel that enough was enough.

The counsel for the defence pleaded to call just one more witness – Admiral Dacres who had served with Lutwidge on the *Endymion.* The judge allowed Dacres to join those who had already extolled Lutwidge's virtues, most of whom, according to *The Times* were '... gallant men who were so agitated in delivering their testimony that several of them found it difficult to articulate'.

Lieutenant Lutwidge then took the stand and, having related his account of the incident, assured the court that he had intended nothing more than to compel a drunken man to yield his place to another, who could discharge that duty which the deceased was utterly unable to perform.

Finally, Mr Justice Le Blanc summed up the case for the jury. He told them that to constitute the crime of murder the circumstances must be such as to indicate a malignant disposition. Every person in authority – master, officer or father – has a right in law to employ some means of force to compel obedience, although obviously the means employed must not be likely to cause death. If excess force was used in the heat of the moment and death ensued, then the person concerned must face the consequences, although he would not be guilty of murder but of homicide.

The jury almost instantly found Lieutenant Lutwidge 'Not Guilty' of murder but 'Guilty' of manslaughter, a verdict that elicited a disbelieving gasp from the many spectators who had packed the courtroom to see the proceedings.

Mr Justice Le Blanc let it be known that the verdict of manslaughter was an appropriate one since Fagan's death had arisen from 'sudden provocation'. However, he believed that the provocation was not sufficient to justify the act and, for this reason, the law required satisfaction. Accordingly, he sentenced Lutwidge to serve a further three months in prison and to pay a fine of £100.

After his release from prison, Lutwidge went back to sea, only to be shipwrecked off the coast of France in 1804. He managed to swim ashore and was promptly captured and sent to a French prison, where he was held until 1814. He was eventually promoted to captain.

But for Lutwidge's admission to hitting Fagan and his insistence to Captain Digby that further enquiries were made, the cause of the Fagan's death would undoubtedly have been attributed to his own drunkenness and Lutwidge would have gone unpunished. Apparently, his conscience would not allow this and the man described as 'an officer and a gentleman on every occasion' was prepared to risk his career and even his life to ensure that justice was seen to be done.

2

'WHO OR WHAT IS IT THE BASTARD WANTS?'

Fareham, 1827

On Saturday, 22 December 1827, labourer John Tatford was walking along Puxall Lane from Fareham to his father's house at Blackbrook when he came across the body of a young man lying in a ditch at the roadside, one leg stretched out into the road. Tatford ran as fast as he could to his father's house and led him and a neighbour back to where the body lay. While John Tatford and the neighbour, Robert Aldridge, stood guard over the body, Mr Henry Tatford went to fetch the police.

Henry Harris accompanied Tatford back to where his son waited and between them the four men lifted the body out of the ditch and carried it to the shelter of a nearby barn. It was a winter's night and the weather was cold and wet, yet the body still retained some vestiges of warmth beneath the arms.

Once the body was safely in the barn it quickly became evident that the young man had suffered some terrible injuries. His throat had been cut so deeply that his head was almost severed from his body. Part of his right ear had been cut off and he had a stab wound on his right cheek. In addition, he had a one-inch wound on the back of his head. A post-mortem examination, carried out by Fareham surgeon Thomas Blatherwick on 24 December, determined that the wound to the man's throat, which was seven inches long, had completely severed the windpipe and all the major blood vessels. In the opinion of the surgeon, death would have been instantaneous and could not have been suicide. He had been murdered.

The young man's identity was soon established. He was William Harmsworth, a labourer who lived with his father near Titchfield and, once the body had been positively identified, there immediately seemed to be an obvious suspect for the murder. Harmsworth's friend, Moses Sheppard, had been drinking with him in both The Sun at Brockenhurst and The Lamb at Fareham on 22 December and the two men had left the latter inn together shortly before Harmsworth's body was found. A Mr Aymore clearly recalled bidding 'Goodnight' to the two men in Fareham and Aymore had the highest credentials as a witness, being a police constable.

Somewhat surprisingly, none of the numerous witnesses who had seen the accused and the victim drinking together had noticed even the slightest signs of any animosity between them – they seemed to have been on the best of terms all night. Yet there had evidently been some recent quarrel between them since, for the past couple of days, Harmsworth, who often went out drinking with Sheppard, had avoided his company. When Sheppard had called for Harmsworth at his lodgings on the day of the murder, Harmsworth had initially asked his landlord, 'Who or what is it the bastard wants?' then refused to go out, although he eventually capitulated.

On the morning of 23 December, PC Aymore and PC Harris went to Sheppard's father's house at Brockenhurst, where they found Sheppard at breakfast. When they told him that they wished to question him about the murder of William Harmsworth, he blanched and became very agitated. As PC Aymore escorted Sheppard to the police station, he reminded him that he had bade him 'Goodnight' in Fareham only the night before. Sheppard initially denied this but eventually admitted that he had in fact spoken to the policeman.

A search of the house at Brockenhurst turned up a greatcoat, which was wet. The lower halves of both sleeves appeared to have been recently washed and wrung out. However, there were still faint traces of a reddish substance on the sleeves, which the police described as being either blood or iron mould. When Sheppard was searched at the police station, a blood-spotted handkerchief and a small clasp knife were removed from his pockets.

An inquest into the death of William Harmsworth was opened before coroner Mr C.H. Longcroft at the Golden Lion Inn, Fareham. The jury was taken to view Harmsworth's body, which still lay in the barn where Constable Harris had placed it.

However, the coroner then requested that the body be brought from the barn to the inn where the inquest was being held so that Sheppard, who had by now been charged with the murder, could view it. Sheppard became terribly agitated at the sight of the body and swore to the coroner that he knew nothing about the murder. The coroner then suggested that, if this were indeed the case, Sheppard should have no objection to laying his hand on the body and saying, 'I am innocent of this murder'.

Sheppard flatly refused to do so. He shrank from the body and became so distressed that he had to be taken to another room in the pub. There was a bed in the room and Sheppard flung himself onto it on the verge of fainting. His face turned almost yellow with fear and he broke out into a cold sweat.

A cottage at Brockenhurst. (Author's collection)

High Street, Fareham.
(Author's collection)

When he had recovered, he was taken back to the inquest where the coroner's jury heard evidence from a number of people about the events of 22 December.

Several people testified to having seen Harmsworth and Sheppard drinking together at The Lamb public house at around nine o'clock on the evening of 22 December. While there, Sheppard had been persuaded to eat some bread and cooked meat and had taken a large knife out of his coat pocket in order to cut a piece from the pork hock. Soon afterwards, Harmsworth had said to Sheppard, 'Come Sheppard, I am going. Are you almost ready to go?' According to the witnesses, Sheppard had seemed reluctant to leave but had eventually walked out of the pub with Harmsworth at just after nine o'clock. He still had the bread, meat and his knife in his hand.

PC Aymore had seen the two men walking in the direction of Puxall Lane, seemingly chatting amicably together. Then, between nine and ten o'clock, Henry Tatford, who lived in a cottage very close to the scene of the murder, heard his dog barking frantically. Tatford went to his door and looked round but saw nothing. He did hear some rustling coming from the hedge but, as there were no cries for help, he assumed that the noises were made by someone cutting foliage to use for Christmas decorations. John Tatford testified to finding the body at just before eleven o'clock.

Constable Harris told the inquest about being summoned to the scene and finding the handle of a clasp knife lying beneath Harmsworth's head. The dead man's pockets still contained 14s 7d – a tidy sum in 1827 – which seemed to suggest that robbery had not been the motive for the murder. Harris went on to describe the greatcoat, knife and handkerchief found when Sheppard was arrested.

Meanwhile, on 22 December, Sheppard had next been seen at the Three Tuns public house in Elson at between ten and eleven o'clock. He arrived at the inn in a state of some excitement, his clothes wet. He had called for beer but such was his demeanour that Mr Speyshott, the landlord, refused to serve him and asked him to leave the pub. He was last seen running towards his father's house.

Sheppard continued to deny all knowledge of the murder, insisting that he had been at his sister's house at the time. However, his sister had already been interviewed and had denied having seen her brother. The coroner offered to have Sheppard's sister brought before the inquest, but Sheppard declined.

The coroner's jury returned a verdict of wilful murder against Moses Sheppard and he was sent to Winchester Gaol to await trial at the Lent Assizes.

The proceedings opened before Mr Justice Gaselee on 7 March 1828. All of the witnesses who had attended the inquest now testified at the trial, the majority of them called by the prosecution. Very few witnesses appeared for the defence, although Sheppard's father and another witness both assured the court that the alleged bloodstains on Sheppard's greatcoat had been ox blood and that his coat had been stained some time before the murder, while he was dressing the head of an ox for his family.

The prosecution then advanced a possible motive for the murder – that of jealousy. Sheppard and Harmsworth had worked together for a builder in Gosport but their employer had been forced to lay off most of his staff for the winter. Harmsworth, a skilled bricklayer, was the only workman retained and this had made his former workmates very bitter towards him and, as one, they had vowed revenge. For most of the men, this had been an idle threat but Sheppard had been more determined than his colleagues and had followed Harmsworth home after hearing the news of his redundancy, all the while swearing at him and threatening him.

If the perceived favouritism at work was not motive enough, the prosecution also produced Mr Richard Gethin as a witness. Sheppard had been in the habit of visiting Gethin's wife and, as it was coyly written in the newspapers of the day, '... the visits were made under such circumstances as left little doubt of the nature of the acquaintance between the prisoner and Mrs Gethin.'

Sheppard had apparently discovered that William Harmsworth had also 'visited' Mrs Gethin and, in a fit of jealous rage, had told Mr Gethin about the 'evil practices' of his wife with Harmsworth, omitting to mention his own lengthy involvement with her. Richard Gethin told the court that, as a result of Sheppard's allegations, he had confronted his wife and, having received satisfactory proof of her infidelity, had turned her out of the house.

Having heard all the evidence, the jury retired for a quarter of an hour before returning a verdict of 'Guilty'. Mr Justice Gaselee ordered that Sheppard be returned to Winchester Gaol to await his execution.

Back in prison, Moses Sheppard once more became very upset and confessed his guilt to the prison chaplain, expressing great remorse for his crime. He acknowledged that jealousy had been the reason that he had decided to kill William Harmsworth and said that he had first hit him on the back of the head with a large stick, knocking him down, before slashing his throat with his knife.

Sheppard was allowed to see his brothers and sisters on the day before his execution then at just after eight o'clock on the morning of Monday, 10 March 1828, he walked to the gallows, seemingly deep in prayer. When the bolt was drawn back, twenty-three-year-old Moses Sheppard struggled briefly for a few moments before finally dying. His body was passed to the prison surgeon for dissection.

Note: Contemporary accounts of the murder give numerous variations of the spelling of the surname of the murderer. He is described as Sheppard, Shephard, Shepard, Shepherd and Shepperd. Since Sheppard seems to be a common Hampshire surname, I have elected to use that spelling for this account.

3

'WHAT THE DEVIL HAVE YOU BEEN UP TO?'

Portsmouth, 1830

William Winney was just one of approximately 500 prisoners housed on board the convict hulk *York* and, by 1830, had already served five years of his fourteen-year sentence. Each day, Winney was taken to the Gun Wharf at Portsmouth, where he worked as a sawyer. Although Winney was a habitual criminal, with several previous convictions for larceny (theft), he was known as an exemplary prisoner. Sober, diligent and hard working, he was considered sufficiently trustworthy by his guards to be elevated to the position of deputy foreman. However, as well as his legitimate labours at the Gun Wharf, Winney also operated a lucrative sideline, of which the guards were either unaware or to which they were prepared to turn a blind eye.

Winney traded in tobacco and spirits, bought surreptitiously on his behalf by one of the regular labourers at the Gun Wharf. In addition, he was known to make loans to his fellow convicts, which he naturally expected to be repaid with interest. Although these transactions were normally only for small amounts of money, Winney had little on which to spend his earnings and gradually accumulated quite a nest egg, which he carried hidden in a primitive flannel money belt, worn wrapped around his body under his clothes.

Shortly after Christmas of 1829, Winney received a letter from his wife informing him of the death of one of their daughters. The letter went on to relate that Winney's wife and family were in a state of near starvation and the words were enough to plunge Winney into a deep depression. He wept in despair as he bemoaned the fact that he could do nothing to help his family, complaining bitterly that he was owed a great deal of money by his fellow convicts, who had either not paid for their contraband or had reneged on payments for loans he had advanced them.

Thus, when Winney was found dead in store number 9 at the Gun Wharf on 15 January 1830, with three cuts across his throat and a bloody knife lying by his side, it was initially assumed that he had committed suicide. Fellow convict John Powell – also known as Langley Pearce – had gone in search of Winney, hoping to purchase a little tobacco from him. In spite of asking several other labourers where Winney might be found, Powell was unable to locate him until he happened to glance into store number 9.

Powell immediately informed warden William Francis Wolfe about his grim discovery and Wolfe sent for a doctor. Once Winney had officially been declared dead, Wolfe arranged for his body to be transported back to the *York*. There the body was washed before any of the ship's surgeons could examine it and give an opinion on the cause of Winney's death. Eventually, surgeons William Hawkings Garrington and his assistant Heziah Prouce inspected the body and, having examined his throat, determined that Winney had bled to death as a result of his self-inflicted injuries.

An inquest was held by the coroner for the Admiralty and, knowing that Winney had been extremely depressed prior to his death, the inquest recorded that Winney died by his own hand, while under the influence of temporary derangement. However, the doctors who had examined Winney after his demise then began to have second thoughts about the manner of his death and quickly came to doubt their own conclusions.

Given that Winney had supposedly cut his own throat three times, it was surprising that there was no blood on his cuffs or on the front of his coat. In addition, the prison ship was buzzing with gossip and rumours about Winney's money. He was known to have possessed at least one gold sovereign and many prisoners believed that he carried at least another four tucked safely away in his money belt.

The doctors examined William Winney again, this time paying particular attention to his money belt, which had been empty when his body was discovered. They found bloody fingerprints on the money belt and, when they took a closer look at his throat, they decided that the direction and depth of his wounds made it highly unlikely that Winney, who had been almost decapitated, could have inflicted them himself. When the doctors originally examined the body, they had noticed a contusion on Winney's left temple, which they had assumed had resulted from his falling heavily to the ground after cutting his throat. Now they found that Winney's skull was fractured beneath the innocuous-looking wound. The fact that there was no blood on the front of the dead man's coat suggested that his throat had been cut while he was lying down. The doctors revised their initial conclusions, now saying that Winney seemed to have been struck on the head with sufficient force to render him unconscious and his throat then cut by another person or persons. Whoever had done this would have had blood on their hands and, in emptying Winney's money belt, had left unmistakeable traces on the cloth.

A second inquest was opened before Portsmouth Borough coroner, Mr Franklin Howard. This time, the coroner's jury could clearly understand that Winney had been murdered, but, to everyone's surprise, their eventual verdict was 'wilful murder against John Powell'.

The evidence against Powell was flimsy – so much so that the coroner himself expressed an opinion after the inquest that Powell was not involved in Winney's death, apart from the indisputable fact that he had found the body. However, Howard could not argue with the verdict of his jury and so had no alternative but to commit Powell for trial at the next assizes on a coroner's warrant.

The evidence that had persuaded the coroner's jury of Powell's guilt came from another convict, William Brown. Powell was known to be in debt to Winney, owing him four pence for tobacco. He insisted that, as soon as he found Winney's body, he ran to alert the guard, Mr Wolfe. Yet William Brown told the inquest that he had seen Powell go into store number 9 and that he had remained there for several minutes before going to fetch Wolfe.

The Gun Wharf at Portsmouth. (Author's collection)

Powell would have had to pass through another shed to get to number 9 and a careful search of this shed had revealed a small leather bag stuffed into the neck of a porter bottle, which was hidden under some gun tracks. Although it was not possible to positively confirm that the bag belonged to Winney, it was found to contain six sovereigns and six shillings and there were a number of blood drops and bloody finger marks on the gun and tracks, some of which appeared to have been partially wiped off. If Powell had murdered Winney, according to Brown's testimony, he had sufficient time alone with him in the shed to knock him unconscious, cut his throat, rifle through his money belt and conceal the money to be retrieved later.

No blood was found on John Powell's clothes and, without Brown's testimony, the most damning evidence against him was that several convicts insisted that Powell had told them that he had dreamed the night before the murder that Charley Willis (another convict) had cut Winney's throat in three places. The accusation of murder against Powell might have been more credible had he been a violent criminal, but he was actually serving his prison sentence for the relatively minor offence of stealing a jacket.

While the prisoners on the *York* were convicts, they were not prepared to see an innocent man go to the gallows for a crime he had not committed and it was brought to the attention of warden John Purcell that Brown himself had been unaccountably absent from the saw pit where he was working at the time of Winney's murder. On 28 January, Purcell confronted Brown, telling him that everyone on the ship suspected that he was involved in Winney's murder and suggesting that he disclosed what he knew about it.

'I am not the person but I know who did it,' Brown admitted, now naming another convict, Smith Williams. According to Brown, Williams had been planning to rob Winney for some weeks but Brown had always believed that Williams intended to 'hocus' Winney (render him unconscious by administering laudanum) rather than kill him. Brown told Purcell that, on the morning of Winney's murder, he had seen Williams coming out of number 9 shed with his hands covered in blood.

'What have you been up to?' he asked him.

'Never mind – hold your tongue – all is right,' Williams replied, heading for the pump where he washed his hands.

Brown followed him to the pump, asking, 'What the devil have you been up to?' Pressed by Brown, Williams eventually confessed to having murdered Winney, saying that he had hidden Winney's money in the neck of a bottle and offering to share the spoils with Brown in exchange for his silence.

With Smith Williams now implicated in Winney's murder, the guards questioned the other members of the party who had been working at the Gun Wharf again and it emerged that both Williams and Brown had been seen talking together shortly before the murder. Both had been unaccountably absent from their work for a few minutes at the crucial time and both had subsequently been seen with blood on their hands and clothes.

In common with all the other members of the working party, both Brown and Williams's clothes had been inspected two days after Winney's death and no traces of blood had been found on the garments of either man. A further examination of the clothes made on the following day again revealed no bloodstains. In the light of the alleged involvement of Williams and Brown in the murder, their clothes were inspected again on 29 January and yet again, no blood was found. However, at that time, the clothes were impounded by ship's carpenter John Strickland, who passed them onto the ship's surgeons for closer scrutiny. Garrington and Prouce believed that they could see traces of blood on the garments of both Brown and Williams, although in Brown's case, the fact that his waistcoat and 'small clothes' were a deep crimson red in colour had rendered the stains almost invisible.

Meanwhile, John Powell appeared at the Lent Assizes in Winchester, charged on the coroner's warrant with the wilful murder of William Winney. His appearance was a mere formality and, in the absence of any evidence offered against him, he was discharged from court and given a King's Pardon, which effectively terminated his incarceration for his original misdemeanour of stealing a jacket.

Smith Williams and William Brown were committed to appear at the next Hampshire Assizes before Mr Baron Bolland, jointly charged with 'having on 15 January last, feloniously made an assault on William Winney in the borough of Portsmouth and him then and there killed and murdered.'

Mr Coleridge, for the prosecution, called a number of convicts as witnesses. John Powell testified to finding the body, while George Gardiner and another convict (whose name is recorded only as Pilkington) testified that Brown had been absent from the saw pit where he was working shortly before the discovery of Winney's murder. Pilkington went on to state that William Brown had approached him prior to his appearance in court and tried to persuade him to give false testimony, a request he had refused. Gardiner also told the court that the knife used to slash Winney's throat belonged to him. He had lost his knife a few weeks before the murder and, since he and Brown shared a store cupboard where they kept their tools, the obvious implication was that Brown had ready access to the murder weapon and could easily have taken it from the locker he shared with its rightful owner.

William Morgan told the court that, on the morning of the murder, he had seen blood on William Brown's hand, as well as spots of blood on his waistcoat, stockings and 'small clothes'. Morgan described the spots of blood as 'larger than a shilling' but stated that he believed that Brown had helped carry Winney's body back to the ship, so could have picked up the bloodstains then.

It was quickly established that Morgan was mistaken in his belief that Brown had assisted in moving the body, which left the murder of Winney as a possible explanation for any blood on his clothes. However, Morgan's evidence of having seen drops bigger than a shilling was in obvious contradiction to the three subsequent examinations of his clothes on board the ship, at which no bloodstains had been observed. Mr Baron Bolland interjected at this point to remind the jury that Brown's clothes were crimson in colour and thus any moisture such as drops of water could have the appearance of bloodstains on his clothing. (Although a perfectly reasonable explanation, it does, of course, fail to account for the blood allegedly observed by Morgan on Brown's hand.)

Finally, William Buck testified that Smith Williams had told him about the existence of a second knife, which had also been used in the murder of William Winney. Buck said that Williams had told him that he had wrapped his own knife in a handkerchief and concealed it in the water pump. When the pump was searched on 2 February, a handkerchief and knife were found exactly as Williams had described, embedded in the frozen water.

Although neither Brown nor Williams was defended, both were allowed to address the court in their own defence.

Brown began by protesting his innocence and complaining that the captain of the *York* had refused some convicts leave to appear at the trial. Had these witnesses been permitted to testify, Brown believed that they would have proved that some of the testimony given by other witnesses was false. Brown explained the presence of blood on his clothes by saying that he suffered from bad headaches and, on occasions, deliberately made his nose bleed as a way of relieving the pains in his head. He asked that George Gardiner be recalled to confirm this statement, which Gardiner duly did. Finally, Brown asked the jury to pay particular attention to the fact that he had not been charged with any offence until it was generally known that any convicts giving evidence against him would be given a King's Pardon and thus be released from their sentences.

Smith Williams also protested his innocence. He too had a ready explanation for any bloodstains found on his clothes, saying that he suffered from frequent nosebleeds that were so severe that, on one occasion, the surgeon at Winchester Gaol had bled him in an effort to divert his blood away from his head.

The protestations of innocence by the two defendants did little to change the minds of the jury who, after a brief deliberation, returned a verdict of 'Guilty of wilful murder' against them both. They were hanged at Winchester Gaol on 26 July 1830, just three days after the conclusion of their trial and their bodies given for dissection.

4

'NOW I'LL TELL YOU THE TRUTH'

Bramdean, near Alresford, 1836

Although he had reached the age of seventy-six, John Hall entertained no thoughts of retiring from the position of letter carrier between Alresford and Bramdean, a job he had held for twenty years. On 19 June 1836, Mr Hall left his home on Bramdean Common at half-past five in the morning to collect the letters from Alresford. His route normally took him through Old Park Wood then on to Bishop's Sutton but, on that particular day, he didn't arrive at Alresford and neither did he return home at the expected time after finishing his work. A search was instigated and, at seven o'clock in the evening, Hall's body was found in a small hollow, screened from the road by bushes at the bottom of Old Park Hill.

Hall had obviously been robbed, although whoever had attacked him had been careful not to steal anything that could be traced back to the letter carrier. His basket and letter bag lay on his chest and his pockets had been turned out and emptied. When Hall left home that morning, he was carrying two half-crowns and two or three shillings but his purse was found empty a few yards away from his body.

The left side of the old man's head had been completely shattered and three large stones found near his body bore traces of blood and hair, as did a large stick, with a crook at one end, which had been discarded in a nearby hedgerow. An inquest was opened into Hall's death by coroner Mr Longcroft and the jury returned a verdict of 'wilful murder by some person or persons unknown'.

The police at Alresford applied to the Home Office for the assistance of a Bow Street Runner and, almost as soon as he arrived in the area, Mr Shackell arrested a suspect for the murder of John Hall.

Sixty-year-old John Deadman was an unemployed waggoner who had fallen on hard times. On 18 June, he visited a shop in Alresford owned by Mr Scorey and related such a tale of woe about having neither money nor food that Scorey gave him three pence, which Deadman immediately spent on drink. Yet, although he was supposedly so destitute that he had told Scorey that he would have to go 'on the parish', on the morning after the murder, Deadman was observed spending money very freely in the local public houses.

Deadman's sudden unexplained wealth attracted the attention of Mr Shackell, who made some discreet enquiries into his movements on 18 and 19 June. When he discovered

Cottages at Bramdean. (Author's collection)

that Deadman had been seen near the scene of the murder and that he was known to own a crooked stick similar to the bloodstained one found in the hedge, Shackell confronted him in a pub in Alresford and arrested him for the wilful murder of John Hall.

John Deadman denied having been in the area at the time of the murder, telling Shackell that he had gone to visit his sister in Petersfield but, on arriving at her house, had been unable to rouse her and had therefore slept in a hedge. Shackell searched his suspect and found a half crown and a farthing in the pocket of his trousers. Asked where he got the money from, Deadman first said that his sister had given it to him but then changed his story, saying that a brother had sent him two shillings and he had begged the remaining money.

Shackell noticed what appeared to be spots of blood on Deadman's boots and stockings and Deadman was also wearing two smocks, the rolled up sleeves of which were heavily bloodstained. At first, Deadman denied that the stains were blood, before conceding that they might be blood from a horse he had bled near Brighton about two months ago. He then changed his explanation again, now saying that the stains could have been made when he wormed a dog.

Shackell advised his prisoner to be cautious in what he was saying, before handing him over to the custody of the Alresford constable, Mr Cooke, who conveyed him to Winchester Gaol.

By the time his case came before Mr Justice Williams at the Winchester Assizes on 9 July 1836, the prosecuting counsels, Mr Greenwood and Mr Dampier, were able to call thirty-two witnesses in support of their case. Williams began the proceedings by asking Deadman if he had appointed any counsel, to which Deadman replied that he had not the means to do so. Williams asked if anyone in court would be prepared to act on the prisoner's behalf and Mr C. Saunders and Mr Poulden stepped forward.

Alresford, c. 1910. (Author's collection)

The prosecution witnesses included a night watchman, Mr Kile, who had been employed overnight between 18 and 19 June to guard some road-works on the Alresford to Petersfield road. Kile told the court that, at about midnight, John Deadman had approached him and told him a sob story about his impoverished circumstances. Eventually, Deadman had walked off towards Bramdean.

A second witness related seeing Deadman passing his house at Bishop's Sutton at half-past two in the morning, heading in the direction of Old Park Wood. Deadman was seen at four o'clock by another witness, this time on the edge of the wood.

At about half-past six that morning, soon after the murder of John Hall was thought to have occurred, Mrs Petts from Ropley saw a man washing his hands in a pond near her home, which was about three-quarters of a mile from the murder scene. The man had taken some time making sure that his hands were clean, giving Mrs Petts a long look at him and she was quite positive that the man was Deadman. A little while later, Deadman was seen by two young boys in Ropley village, where he later struck up a conversation with a Mr Turner, telling him that his name was 'Black Jack Deadman' and that he was lost.

Deadman then went to a beer shop, after which he visited The Checkers public house, where he spent eleven pence. While he was there, a little girl noticed some blood on the sleeve of his smock, which he quickly rolled up when he saw her looking.

From Ropley, Deadman hitched a lift to Southampton with a waggoner and his mate, stopping at The Vine public house on the way. There, landlord Mr Crosswell observed that the murder of the old postman was a terrible thing.

'Yes' agreed Deadman's companion. 'And do you know who they suspect?' he asked, pointing at Deadman.

'How came they to judge me when I was in another part of the country at the time?' asked Deadman rhetorically.

The key witness at the trial was a man named James Lawes, who had been in custody with Deadman in Winchester Prison. Lawes was a habitual criminal who, in 1826, had been transported for seven years for larceny and was now in custody on a charge of stealing some bacon. Lawes told the court that he had struck up a conversation with Deadman in the prison yard and that Deadman had told him that two smock frocks taken from him, as they were covered in blood. 'Now I'll tell you the truth,' Deadman allegedly told Lawes, 'I was the man who knocked him down with a stick and then knocked his brains out with a flint stone and threw him into a hedgerow.'

Hearing this evidence, Deadman's face flushed crimson, before completely draining of all colour. His defence counsel tried to undermine Lawes' evidence by reminding the court of his criminal past and asking why he had not immediately brought the revelation to the attention of the authorities. The charge against Lawes had eventually been dropped and it was only on his release from prison that he spoke out about what Deadman had told him.

Lawes swore that, on the same day as Deadman spoke to him, he had related the conversation to a woman named Mary Carter who, when called to the witness stand, corroborated his account.

Given the opportunity to speak before the judge summed up the case for the jury, John Deadman dismissed Lawes' evidence as false, continuing to insist that he had been out of the area when the murder was committed. However, since he was unable to prove his whereabouts at the time, the jury needed only a short deliberation to pronounce him 'Guilty'.

Deadman heard the pronunciation of his death sentence without flinching and awaited his execution in the condemned cell at Winchester with no apparent anxiety or apprehension. Repeatedly urged to confess his guilt as the first steps towards forgiveness by '... the judge before whom he was shortly to appear', Deadman was executed on 15 July 1836 and maintained his innocence to his last breath. However, it was reported in the local newspapers of the time 'It may be satisfactory to the public to know that, although he didn't confess his crime, he gave sufficient evidence to those immediately concerned with him to leave no doubt of his guilt.'

Note: The owner of the shop in Alresford is alternatively named Mr Scoley in some accounts of the murder in contemporary newspapers, while the night watchman is alternatively named Mr Kill.

5

'I WILL SHOOT HIM LIKE A PARTRIDGE'

When Captain James Alexander Seton and his wife attended an April Ball in Portsmouth in 1845, they met Henry Charles Morehead Hawkey and his wife who was, by all accounts, a very beautiful woman. Initially, the two couples seemed to hit it off and, within days of their first meeting, Seton invited the Hawkeys to dine at his house. However, for Seton, the extension of the hand of friendship towards the Hawkeys had an ulterior motive – as his wife and Henry Hawkey chatted politely after dinner, Seton managed to inveigle a few moments alone with Mrs Hawkey and made a proposition to her that would have been truly shocking to a respectable married woman of the time. Naturally, Mrs Hawkey turned him down in no uncertain terms – even though he did offer her a ring in exchange for her virtue – and, no doubt thinking that she had dealt with the situation, did not mention Seton's improper advances to her husband.

Seton was undeterred by the refusal and, if anything, being spurned prompted him to try even harder to seduce poor Mrs Hawkey. Over the following weeks, he took to visiting her at her lodgings in King's Terrace, Southsea, usually when her husband was on duty as a lieutenant with the Royal Marine Corps.

Mrs Hawkey was still reluctant to mention Seton's unwelcome attentions to her husband, although she did ask her landlady, Mary Ann Stansmore, to tell Seton that she was out when he came calling, telling her that she was afraid of him and calling him 'that horrible old Seton'.

By now, Seton had increased his offer for her virtue to include £100 as well as the aforementioned ring. Anxious to be rid of him, Mrs Hawkey announced her intention to go and stay with her mother who lived near Maidstone. Seton was delighted with this idea as he had a friend who lived there and would be able to stay nearby, giving him the opportunity to get closer to the object of his lust, far away from the inconvenient presence of her husband.

Mr Hawkey was still totally unaware of Seton's inappropriate advances towards his wife and the two couples continued to meet socially, being patrons of King's Rooms on the seafront at Southsea. Hawkey and Seton met there almost every day and seemed to be on very friendly terms. Each man would sometimes partner the other's wife on the dance floor. For Hawkey, dancing with Mrs Seton was nothing more than being sociable, but for Seton, a dance with Mrs Hawkey meant another chance for whispered attempts at seduction. Eventually, Hawkey became suspicious and confronted his wife, who finally told him about Seton's unwelcome attentions.

Whether Mrs Hawkey downplayed the extent of Seton's constant attempts to seduce her is not known, but Hawkey didn't immediately confront his wife's tormentor. Instead he went to speak to their landlady, telling her that if Seton came to visit his wife, she should make frequent excuses to go into the room and on no account leave Seton alone with his wife for too long. Furthermore, if Mrs Hawkey should ring her bell then Mrs Stansmore should go immediately to her assistance.

On 19 May 1845, the Hawkeys and the Setons attended a grand soiree at the King's Rooms. Although the four still seemed to be on friendly terms, Mrs Hawkey seemed reluctant to dance with Seton. She eventually agreed to partner him in a set of quadrilles, since it was not a dance that demanded close contact between the dancers. One dance was not enough for Seton and, as soon as the first set had finished, he asked Mrs Hawkey to join him for a second. At this, Lieutenant Hawkey's patience finally snapped. He ordered Seton to the privacy of a card room and, when Seton joined him there, Hawkey let rip. Telling Seton that he was a blackguard, a scoundrel and a rascal, he then challenged him to a duel, saying that if Seton wouldn't allow him this satisfaction then he would horsewhip him up and down the High Street.

Seton seemed genuinely puzzled at Hawkey's outburst and demanded to know the reason for the lieutenant's challenge. Hawkey was beyond rational explanations and continued to rant at Seton, who eventually left the room to speak to a friend, Lieutenant Byron Rowles.

Rowles sought out another Royal Marines officer and tried to persuade him to intercede in the argument but there was simply no placating Henry Hawkey. Having insisted to his fellow officer that he had not only been insulted, but also injured by Seton, he further demonstrated his anger by delivering a kick to Seton's ample backside. Riled by the public insult, Seton finally agreed to meet him in a duel.

The following morning Byron Rowles called at Hawkey's home in his capacity as Seton's appointed second. Hawkey chose another lieutenant, Edward Pym, as his second and then set about procuring a set of duelling pistols.

It was highly irregular for one of the combatants to be allowed to obtain the weapons but doubtless neither man was fully conversant with the etiquette of fighting a duel. Hawkey first went to Sherwood's, a gunsmith on High Street, Portsmouth and, after firing a few test shots in the shooting gallery, asked the proprietor if he might borrow a pair of pistols. When his request was refused, Hawkey went to Thomas Fiske's shop, where he again asked to borrow a pair of pistols. Again, he was turned down and eventually he was forced to part with ten guineas in order to purchase them.

As soon as he had bought them, he went back to Sherwood's accompanied by his second and fired a few practice shots from both pistols. Having selected the weapon he preferred, he borrowed a tool and scratched a small cross on it. Well satisfied with his morning's work, he gloated to Pym, 'I will shoot him like a partridge.'

Later that day, Pym and Hawkey took the ferry from Portsmouth to Gosport, accompanied by a marine private, William Marsh, who acted as a servant to Lieutenant Pym. Marsh carried the pistols in a mahogany case wrapped in brown paper.

On landing at Gosport, the three men disembarked and made their way on foot to Browndown, the agreed meeting place. It had been chosen as the perfect place for the duel since it was isolated and the participants were unlikely to attract the attention of any passers-by. At Browndown, Hawkey and Pym went on alone, leaving Marsh to wait on the shingle beach, his view of the proceedings obscured by a large bank.

The two combatants took their weapons and retreated to a distance of fifteen yards. Seton was first to fire but his shot went wide of his target. Hawkey then raised his pistol but it misfired, probably because Pym was unfamiliar with the loading mechanism and had failed to load it correctly.

With both men having fired one shot, there was a perfect opportunity for them to declare honour satisfied. There was also a chance for the two seconds to intervene, but nothing was said and the duellers took aim again. Once more, Seton fired and missed, but Hawkey, who fired almost simultaneously, was luckier. Seton was a fat man and presented a sizeable target, even though he had turned sideways in an effort to minimise the proportion of his body visible to his opponent. Hawkey's second bullet hit the right-hand side of Seton's rotund belly, travelling through his body and exiting his left groin.

The two seconds had neglected to arrange for any medical assistance to be present so Hawkey and Rowles tried to staunch the flow of blood from Seton's wounds while Pym ran back along the beach to where Marsh was waiting, sending him back to Gosport to fetch a doctor. When Pym returned, he and Hawkey took to their heels and ran the three miles back to Gosport. After spending the night there they went into hiding, possibly in France.

John Jenkins, the surgeon, arrived from Gosport and Seton was given emergency medical treatment. Jenkins found Seton to be in a weakened condition, close to fainting, his pulse barely perceptible. He had a wound caused by a pistol ball on his right hip, a badly swollen groin and scrotum and appeared to have lost a lot of blood. Having partially revived him with brandy and water, Jenkins washed and dressed his wounds. Assisted by two coastguards from the Stokes Bay station, Seton was taken aboard a yacht, *Dream*, and transported to Portsmouth, where he was sent to the Quebec Hotel and put to bed, with instructions to rest. Mr Jenkins stayed with him for two hours until it seemed that the crisis point had passed and Seton might survive.

Attended every day by surgeons, Seton initially appeared to be making good progress, but after a week his doctors became concerned that he may be suffering from internal bleeding, having observed what they described as a 'pulsating tumour'. Despite applying ice and cold packs to the tumour, it gradually increased in size and the doctors attending Seton feared that it might burst at any moment. Deciding that an operation to tie the artery supplying the tumour with blood was the only possible course of action, the local surgeons sent to London for Mr Robert Liston who consented to perform the operation assisted by two more London surgeons, George Sampson and J.P. Potter.

Seton was told of the seriousness of his condition and made a deposition describing the duel and stating that it was Lieutenant Hawkey who had fired the pistol at him, causing his injury. He still seemed totally unable to comprehend what had driven Hawkey to challenge him to a duel in the first place saying, 'I am perfectly innocent. If I were to die this moment, I know not why I was shot.' On 31 May, an operation was performed to tie off Seton's iliac artery. Although severely hampered by Seton's obesity, the surgeons deemed the operation to have been a success. However, Seton grew progressively weaker and eventually died two days later.

The trial of Lieutenant Pym at Winchester, 1846. (Author's collection)

James Allan, a surgeon from the Haslar Naval Hospital, carried out a post-mortem examination. While agreeing that Seton's gunshot wound was life threatening, Allan was unable to state whether he had died as a direct result of the wound or because of the operation to tie off the artery.

There was public outrage at Seton's death and Pym and Hawkey stayed in hiding until they believed that the ill-feeling against them had died down. Only then did Pym surrender himself to the police. He was tried at Winchester Assizes in March 1846, charged with aiding and abetting Lieutenant Hawkey in the wilful murder of James Seton.

The laws concerning duelling in England were straightforward. If a person was killed while fighting a duel then everyone present, whether the other protagonist or a second, could be found guilty of wilful murder. The armed forces also took a very dim view of the practice and proposing a duel, assisting with one or even failing to prevent one attracted stiff penalties. Thus Pym's trial should have been an open and shut case but, to everyone's surprise, the jury deliberated for less than three minutes before returning a verdict of 'Not Guilty'.

At the conclusion of the trial, Mr Serjeant Cockburn, who had defended Pym, approached the judge and informed him that Hawkey was willing to give himself up, provided he could be tried at this assizes. 'Let him wait', said Mr Justice Earle and thus Hawkey was brought for trial at the next Winchester Assizes in July 1846.

He was charged with the wilful murder of James Seton '... by shooting him with a pistol loaded with a leaden bullet and giving him a mortal wound on the right side', to which he pleaded not guilty. Mr Serjeant Cockburn was once again appointed counsel for the defence and once more he did a sterling job of bamboozling the jury with a two-hour long speech, at the conclusion of which he stated that the accusation against his client was unfounded since Seton had died as a result of the operation not because of the gunshot wound.

The judge, Mr Baron Platt, refuted many of the defence's arguments in his summing up of the case for the jury, but to no avail. The jury barely bothered to deliberate and immediately returned a verdict of 'Not Guilty', at which the court erupted. The police struggled to maintain order as Hawkey was escorted from the court to freedom, to the delight of the many naval officers who had attended the trial, while the carriage in which the trial judge left the court was greeted with loud cheers and applause.

Although it obviously wasn't known at the time, the duel between Henry Charles Morehead Hawkey and James Alexander Seton was to be the last recorded fatal duel ever to be fought in England.

6

'I HAVE DONE FOR YOUR FANCY OLD BASTARD AFTER ALL'

Romsey, 1851

On Thursday, 13 November 1851, fifty-five-year-old farmer John Soffe made a regular trip into Romsey with his horse and cart, intending to get some corn ground into flour at the town mill. Unusually, he didn't return home that evening and, when there was no sign of him the following morning, his brother travelled to Romsey to make some enquiries. The horse that Soffe had been driving was a young and slightly unpredictable animal and there was obvious concern that the farmer might have met with an accident.

At Romsey, Soffe learned that his brother had deposited the corn at the mill at eleven o'clock in the morning, promising to return to collect it between three and four o'clock that afternoon. On learning that the bran and flour had indeed been collected as arranged, Soffe's brother returned home to Minstead, hoping to find John there waiting for him. However, there was still no sign of John Soffe, so on the following morning, his brother and John's son, George, went back to Romsey. It was here that they were told that a hat had been found floating in the River Test between the bridge and Sadler's Mill and, in addition, an empty canvas purse had been picked up on the causeway adjoining the river. George recognised both the hat and purse as belonging to his father.

The police were called and a search was begun for the missing man. On the following morning, his body was found lying on the bottom of the river at Pearce's Meadow, in a secluded spot a long way from any public paths or roads.

The body was conveyed to the Lamb Inn at Romsey, where the man's pockets were turned out and found to be almost empty. The coroner was informed about the death and immediately ordered a post-mortem examination, which was conducted by Mr Wiltshire, a Romsey surgeon. Wiltshire found the body to be that of a strong, well-built man, whose organs were all perfectly healthy, with the exception of the lungs and brain. These showed evidence of congestion, leading Wiltshire to conclude that the man had died from drowning. He found absolutely no marks of violence on the body and yet nothing to suggest that the man had died from natural causes.

The police immediately began to trace John Soffe's movements on his visit to Romsey. They established that, after dropping his corn at the mill, he had driven into town and left his horse and cart at the premises of Charles Bailey, a beer seller in Middlebridge Street, where he ate a meal of bread and ham in the company of two young men. At just after two o'clock, Soffe had been seen in Hog Lane playing with some children, in the company of two young women. At that time, he was described as being 'rather the worse for liquor'.

By half-past three, he had returned to Bailey's, still with the two women, and they had all eaten more bread and ham and drunk more beer. He had collected his goods from the mill, paying the sum of 2s 3d in coins, which he removed from a rather dirty red canvas purse. The miller, Mr Matthews, noted that the purse was bulging with coins, some gold, some silver and that, after making his payment, Soffe replaced his purse in the left-hand pocket of his breeches. He also told police that Soffe had evidently been drinking and was quite tipsy.

After leaving the mill, Soffe returned to Romsey, tethering his horse and cart outside Bailey's and taking a seat in the taproom. He was shortly joined by the two men and two women he had been seen with earlier in the day and the five shared a quart of beer.

When that had been drunk, Soffe went to the bar to order another quart, but the landlord was reluctant to sell him any more in view of his drunken state. He was eventually persuaded to allow Soffe just one more quart, which was again shared with his four companions. At half-past four, all five left the beer house. Soffe was well known to the landlord, as was his heavy drinking, and Bailey escorted Soffe outside, describing him as drunk, but not as drunk as he had been in the past when he had frequently been unable to mount his cart without assistance. On this occasion, Soffe just about managed to climb up onto the cart and sat, swaying slightly, while Bailey untied his horse for him.

Seeing that the four people with whom Soffe had been drinking were still loitering about, Bailey warned Soffe about them and suggested that Soffe should leave his purse with him for safekeeping. Soffe demurred, telling the landlord that he was going straight home, so Bailey led the cart a little way towards the bridge and then watched as Soffe drove slowly away.

Minstead village, 1961. (Author's collection)

Middle Bridge and Broadlands, Romsey. (Author's collection)

The Market Place, Romsey, 1950s. (Author's collection)

Some people living on the other side of the bridge had watched Soffe's progress for several minutes. They saw two young women chasing after the cart, shouting at Soffe to stop and buy them some more beer. They also saw two young men lurking in the shadows outside the Bridge Inn. Eventually, Soffe stopped his horse and cart and was helped down by the two women who led him into the pub. They were quickly followed by the two men.

The party ordered beer, paid for by Soffe, and soon became very rowdy. An argument developed between Soffe and one of the young men about a shilling, which the man obviously believed that Soffe owed him for binding some leather some time previously. The argument became so noisy that the landlord, William Webb, threatened to throw them out if they didn't quieten down.

The two women left the pub at about six o'clock followed shortly afterwards by John Soffe, then a little later by the two men. Soon afterwards, Charles Bailey spotted one of the men leading Soffe's horse and cart by his pub. Bailey asked the man what he intended to do with the horse and cart and what had happened to Mr Soffe, to which the man replied that he was taking the horse up the street and that he didn't know where Soffe was.

Bailey insisted on stabling the horse at his pub and waited up until half-past twelve at night, fully expecting Soffe to return and collect it. Meanwhile, the young man returned to the Bridge Inn where he ordered yet more beer. As he drank, he repeatedly told the landlord 'I know a thing or two' but, when Webb asked him what he meant, he refused to elaborate, saying that Webb would hear something in the morning.

Both Charles Bailey and William Webb knew the identity of Soffe's four companions and identified them to the police as John Eyres, John Kemish, Emma Leach and Mary Ann Simms. An inquest into the death of John Soffe had recorded a verdict of wilful murder and, as the last four people known to have seen Soffe alive, Eyres, Kemish, Leach and Simms were promptly arrested and charged with his murder.

Their trial opened before Mr Justice Talfourd at Winchester on 5 March 1852. Only Eyres and Kemish were tried, although Simms and Leach were still imprisoned at the time of the trial and appeared as witnesses for the prosecution. This was conducted by Mr C. Saunders and Mr Cooke, while Mr Sewell and Mr Prideaux handled the defence of the two accused.

Having viewed a plan of the area where Soffe's body had been found, in just two feet of water, the court then heard from Mr Matthews, the miller, who testified to the events of 13 November. Next to take the witness stand was eighteen-year-old Emma Leach. Leach said that she had first seen Mr Soffe in Hog Lane on the afternoon of 13 November. He had been leaning against a wall, watching Mary Ann Simms, who was playing with some children.

According to Emma Leach, Soffe then beckoned Mary Ann to follow him. Mary Ann had her child with her and, obviously thinking that she might need someone to look after the child while she was otherwise engaged, asked Emma to accompany her.

The two women went with Soffe to Bailey's public house, where Soffe bought beer and cakes before leaving them for about half an hour, presumably to collect his flour. He then returned and bought another quart of beer and some bread and ham.

At this point, John Kemish and John Eyres had come into the pub and Eyres asked Soffe for a shilling, which he seemed to think that Soffe owed him for some work he had done for him. Soffe had first ignored Eyres, but when he persisted, had promised to stand him a quart of beer, with another to follow. The four had drunk beer and eaten bread and ham until, according to Emma Leach, Soffe had offered Mary Ann two shillings to go up the lane with him.

Mary Ann had agreed, but told Soffe that she would need to pay Emma something for looking after her child while she did so. Soffe had handed Emma a shilling, at which Eyres had become quite annoyed, saying that the shilling should be given to him, since he was owed it.

They then moved to the Bridge Inn, where more beer was bought and drunk before Soffe left with Mary Ann, while Emma Leach lingered behind with Mary Ann's child, talking to the landlord's wife and eventually walking with her to her lodgings about 250 yards away. She then walked back and forth with the child in her arms, waiting for Mary Ann to return, which she did after about twenty minutes. The two young women walked back to Mary Ann's house where they parted, having first agreed to have a spending spree that evening.

Emma said that she had not seen Eyres and Kemish again until the following day, when Eyres approached her and said, 'I have done for your fancy old bastard after all.' Kemish had not spoken, although he had nudged Eyres.

Under cross-examination, Emma denied being a streetwalker, but admitted getting into bad company. She told the court that she had been in a church before and knew that there was a God who heard every word she said and that there was a punishment for speaking falsely.

Emma insisted that, although she knew Mary Ann Simms, the two hadn't been particularly close friends and that the outing with Soffe was the very first time that the two had been out together drinking with men.

Mary Ann Simms, who was twenty-three years old, was next to take the stand. Initially, her testimony concurred with Emma Leach's, although Mary Ann maintained that it was Emma that Soffe had invited to go 'up the lane' with him and that she had been there to look after Emma's child. Mary Ann said that she had not been feeling very well and had not wanted to go with Soffe, but that eventually she and Emma had followed him to the Bridge Inn where, after imbibing several quarts of beer with Soffe, Leach, Eyres and Kemish, she had allowed herself to be persuaded to go up the road with Soffe, who had given her two shillings for doing so.

Mary Ann had passed her seven-year-old child to Emma and walked off along the causeway with John Soffe. They talked as they walked, with Mary Ann having to speak quite loudly on account of Soffe being somewhat deaf.

Suddenly, John Eyres came running out of the darkness and told Mary Ann to get out of the way as he intended to have everything the old bastard had. Mary Ann protested, telling Eyres to leave Soffe alone or she would have him 'taken up' when they got back to Romsey. However, Eyres gave her a shove, which knocked her over and began tussling with John Soffe.

Mary Ann told the court that she had seen Eyres take something from Soffe's pocket, which he had then placed in his own pocket. Soffe struggled with Eyres, saying that, were he a younger man, he would fight him properly. Mary Ann again saw Eyres dip into Soffe's pocket and remove a bundle of coins, which he again pocketed. Finally, the scuffle ended with Soffe saying that he would ruin Eyres. Soffe's hat had fallen off in the struggle and he had asked Mary Ann to pick it up for him. As she took it to him, she had heard Eyres saying that Kemish had got Soffe's horse and cart and that he would take Soffe to it.

Mary Ann had asked Eyres if he had not robbed Soffe enough, without leading him away to rob him more, at which Eyres had told her to shut her mouth and pushed her down again. He then whistled to summon John Kemish.

When Kemish arrived, Eyres told him, 'I have got some and intend to have all the old bastard has got.' Mary Ann told the court that she had cried and begged the two men to leave Soffe alone but that Eyres had threatened to stab her if she didn't shut up. Soffe was now threatening to set his son on Eyres and Kemish and the two men had each seized one of his arms and propelled him through the meadow towards the river.

Mary Ann had followed them, begging them to let Soffe go, but they had pushed her over again. At one stage, Soffe had broken free from their grasp, but they had soon recaptured him and she had then heard a loud splash. She had called out 'Murder!' and hallooed, at which Eyres told Kemish 'Fling her in too.' At that, Mary Ann had taken to her heels and fled, not stopping until she had found Emma Leach.

A series of witnesses, including Charles Bailey and William Webb and several of their customers, followed, recounting the events of 13 November. (One customer, Harriet Barnett caused a ripple of laughter in court when she stated, 'I am not a prostitute. I never have been, that I remember anyway.')

James Spearing told of finding Soffe's purse on the 14 November, while Mr Floyd related how he had found the hat in the river and John Pearce recounted helping to remove Soffe's body from the river and taking it to the Lamb Inn. Constable Stephen Ayles told the court how he had found Soffe's body in the river and that, while he was searching, he had been aware of Eyres and Kemish among the crowd of people watching the search from the riverbank. It had been pointed out to him that these were the two men who had been seen with Soffe before his death and he had subsequently arrested them and taken them to the police station for questioning.

Two children were called as witnesses, the first being a twelve-year-old who had heard two men shouting 'Lay hold of the old bastard' at about six or seven o'clock on the evening of Soffe's disappearance. At the same time, he had heard a woman screaming. His mother followed him into the witness box to confirm that he had told her what he had heard and that he had been very agitated about it.

The second child was eleven-year-old Charles Dyott who had seen Eyres and Kemish appearing through the hedge near where to Soffe's body was eventually found early on the morning of 14 November, then again on 15 November.

Finally numerous witnesses were called to testify that both Eyres and Kemish had been freely spending money – most of it on beer – immediately after Soffe had disappeared. One witness, William Rose, had even heard them say, 'Let's go and have a drop of drink now we've done away with the old bastard.'

The evidence against Eyres and Kemish was convincing and it didn't take long for the jury to return a verdict of 'Guilty of murder' against them both. The judge sentenced both men to be executed, but an appeal was immediately launched on the grounds that much of the case for the prosecution rested on the testimony of 'women of bad character', which cast grave doubts on their convictions.

Eventually both men were reprieved and their sentences commuted to life imprisonment. Emma Leach and Mary Ann Simms were subsequently acquitted of any involvement with the murder.

Note: The Bridge Inn is alternatively named the Bridge Tavern in some accounts of the murder and Mary Ann Simms' name is frequently given as Sims. Minstead is alternatively spelled Minestead.

7

'IF I AM NOT GREATLY MISTAKEN, IT WAS A MAN WITH PLENTY OF MONEY AND A VERY BAD WIFE'

Andover, 1858

Henry Edward Northover was employed as an assistant to William Parsons, a draper, tailor and women's outfitter, who kept a large shop on High Street in Andover. He was expected to work long hours and, since he also lived over the premises, he had got into the habit of taking an early morning walk every day to get a little fresh air and a brief peek at life outside the four walls of the shop.

On Tuesday, 23 November 1858, Northover left the shop at half-past seven in the morning and walked out of town on Salisbury Road. He was on the point of turning for home when something unusual caught his eye. Lying in a field at the side of the road was what looked from a distance like a large bundle of rags.

His curiosity piqued, Northover found a gap in the hedge and wriggled through. As he approached the bundle, he was shocked to see that it was actually the body of a man lying face down on the frosted grass, the back of his skull smashed like an eggshell.

Northover didn't stop to investigate more closely but ran as fast as he could back to town. Pausing briefly at the shop to explain to chief assistant Mr Lentall why he would be late for work, he then hurried to summon the police.

Superintendent Charles Wedge and Constable George Abbott accompanied Northover back to the field where he was in for yet another terrible shock. When the body was turned over and he saw the man's face, he immediately recognised the body as being that of his employer, William Parsons.

The two police officers sent for a surgeon and, while they were waiting for him to arrive, they began a search of the area surrounding the body. They found a freshly cut ash stick lying about two feet away, which was roughly a yard long and thicker than a man's wrist. One end of the stick was covered in congealed blood and hair and the officers surmised that this was the murder weapon. There was a cowshed on the edge of the field and footprints on the frosty grass led from the body to the cowshed. Inside the shed, the earth floor showed a number of scuffed footprints and some of the chalk had fallen off the inner walls as though a recent struggle had taken place there.

High Street, Andover, 1914. (Author's collection)

Salisbury Road, Andover. (Author's collection)

The search was interrupted by the arrival of the surgeon Mr Jabez Henry Elliot and a local doctor, Dr William Langstaff. The two doctors examined the dead man, who lay on the grass in a large pool of blood, his clothes covered in frost. The body was stiff and cold and the doctors determined that his death had taken place some hours ago, but were unable to offer a more precise estimate. The man's face was covered in blood and his nose had been broken. He had several severe wounds to the top and back of his head, most with corresponding skull fractures. Elliot believed that some of the wounds were of sufficient severity to stun Parsons but those that had actually fractured his skull would have been responsible for his death. He theorised that a great deal of violence had been used on Mr Parsons, much of it occurring when the deceased was lying on the ground. The body was later removed to a nearby workhouse, where the dead man's pockets were searched. They were found to contain £3 12s 6d, a silver watch with a gold watch chain, a pocketbook, a gold eye-glass and various papers. The police concluded that, whatever the motive for Parsons' murder, it had not been robbery.

The scene of the crime drew many curious onlookers and one, nine-year-old Henry Day, found several coins in the area surrounding the cowshed. Rather than pocketing the coins, Day was honest enough to point them out to the police who eventually picked up six pennies and two halfpennies. This suggested that a scuffle between Parson and his assailant(s) had begun in the cowshed and continued outside and that either Parsons or his attacker(s) had dropped the money. Parsons had probably been trying to escape when he was caught in the middle of the field and fatally beaten.

When Mrs Parsons was contacted, she told police that her husband had left home supposedly to go to the post office, which was almost opposite his house. When he hadn't returned within a few minutes, she assumed that he had met an acquaintance and gone to one of the local public houses for a drink. Strangely enough Parsons was not wearing his own overcoat, but had slipped on a greatcoat that a customer had sent in for repair.

However, while Mrs Parsons believed that her husband had merely gone out to post a letter, the town gossips had a different theory. Allegedly, Parsons was known by everyone except his wife to have an eye for the ladies and it was rumoured that he had in fact left home for a planned liaison with a woman. He had certainly been seen by a witness, Mr Henry Hayes, hurrying away from town at about half-past nine on the evening of his murder.

An inquest into the death of William Parsons was opened on the following day before coroner Harry Footer, who coincidentally owned the field in which Parsons' body had been found. After hearing evidence from Henry Northover, Superintendent Wedge, Mr Elliot the surgeon and Henry Hayes, the coroner adjourned the inquest until 27 November to allow the police more time to investigate.

By the time the inquest reassembled, Mr Elliot had completed his post-mortem examination and reported that, apart from a slight graze on Parsons' left knee and bruising to the left forearm, there was little sign of any injury to the body apart from the head wounds.

Sergeant John Reeves had located the source of the murder weapon, finding a place in the hedge where a tree trunk had been cut. A little further along the hedgerow, the top of the tree had been stuck into the earth, almost as if it had been planted. Both the stump and the top of the tree perfectly matched the cuts at each end of the murder weapon, but to make absolutely certain, Thomas Mesh, a woodman for forty years, was asked to confirm that both the staff and the stump were about eight years old and that the staff had definitely been cut from that tree.

The police had also traced three people who had all heard something on the night of the murder. Thomas Weeks, a corn merchant, had heard what he described as 'a tremendous outcry' that sounded as though it were made by two voices. The noise faded within seconds but shortly afterwards, Weeks heard another sound, which he described as being like somebody repeatedly beating a carpet. By estimating the distance that he had walked against the times he had heard various clocks striking along his route, Weeks estimated that it would have been about 9.40 p.m. when he first heard the shouts.

Next came Mary Hawkins, a laundry worker, who had left work to walk home at about 9.30 p.m. Mrs Hawkins had heard someone 'hallooing' in the distance. She had stopped to listen and had then clearly heard someone say, 'Oh, don't. Don't murder me!'

Ruth Brown, a colleague of Mary Hawkins, had left work at the same time but walked home in the opposite direction. She had clearly heard the words 'Don't ee pray!' followed by a shout of 'Murder!' which was repeated three times. All three witnesses thought the sounds had come from the direction of the Salisbury Road but none had thought to investigate further.

The inquest closed later that day, with a verdict of 'wilful murder against some person or persons unknown' and Parsons' funeral was held that afternoon. However, what didn't emerge at the inquest was that the police had already made an arrest and actually had a suspect in custody.

On Friday 26 November, Thomas and Emma Banks had been holding a birthday party for their two-year-old daughter when the police gatecrashed the event and arrested Thomas for the murder of William Parsons.

Thomas Banks, like Parsons, was a businessman, being the owner of a local public house, The Chequers, as well as having built and rented out several cottages in the town. He was taken before magistrates at the Town Hall in Andover. The hearing was postponed for a week to allow Banks time to consult with Mr Poland, his legal representative and by the time it was resumed, two more witnesses had come forward to say that they too had heard unusual noises on the night of the murder. One, George Pearse, had heard four or five blows, which he too likened to the sound of a carpet being beaten. Pearse had heard no words spoken, but his companion, George Butcher, believed her had heard the word 'Murder!' shouted two or three times, although he admitted the words were indistinct.

Other people had seen Thomas Banks out and about on the night of the murder and again near Mr Footer's field early on the morning after the murder, when he was supposedly walking his dog.

The hearing was again adjourned for a week and by the time it resumed Emma Banks had also been arrested and charged with being an accomplice to the murder of William Parsons. The first witness to testify was a servant girl, Eliza Wiltshire, who worked at a house close to where the Banks family lived. Eliza told the court that, on the night of the murder, she saw Thomas and Emma returning home at between 10.15 and 10.30 p.m. The couple appeared to be quarrelling, although Eliza couldn't hear what was being said.

However, it was the next witness, sixteen-year-old Francis James Webb, who appeared to hold the key to the case.

William Parsons had employed Webb about nine months earlier as a shop assistant. On 21 October, a heavily pregnant Emma Banks had visited the shop to buy a scarf and to look at some dresses. A selection was brought out for her to inspect, but she was unable to find one that she liked, so Webb was sent upstairs to fetch more. When he returned to his counter he realised that one of the first lot of dresses was missing – he particularly noticed it, as it had what he described as 'a peculiar pattern'.

Webb went straight to Mr Lentall, his supervisor, then returned to his counter where he took 2s 6d from Emma Banks in payment for a scarf. As she went to leave the shop, she was stopped just inside the door by Mr Lentall and Mr Parsons. Francis Webb then became involved in dealing with other customers and didn't see any more of the confrontation between his bosses and Mrs Banks. However, half an hour later, he noticed that the dress had been returned and that Mr Parsons had written his own name on the ticket on the back of it.

According to Francis Webb, there followed several days of intrigue and secret meetings with himself acting as a go-between for Emma Banks and Mr Parsons. Emma appeared terrified that people would find out that she had taken a dress and tried to get Webb to arrange a meeting to discuss an explanation that she could give to her husband. She was also concerned about what people would think if they saw her talking to a shop assistant and suggested that she and Webb should meet in a more discreet place.

Webb duly conveyed the details back to William Parsons who would obviously just as soon have forgotten about the whole incident. He was certainly not willing to concoct a story for Thomas Banks as Emma wished him to do. This was relayed to Emma, who begged Webb to arrange a meeting between her and Parsons. If Parsons wouldn't meet her, then she asked if he would say that there had been several parcels on the counter and that she had picked up the dress by mistake. Parsons refused to meet Emma, but did agree to back her up if she wanted to give that version of events to her husband. Although he had not reported the incident of the missing dress to the police, Parsons had mentioned it to his wife. The Parsons' servants got to hear about it and soon there was gossip all over the town.

On the following day, Webb was walking through Andover when Emma Banks's maid ran after him and told him that Mrs Banks wished to see him. Now Emma told him that her husband had gone to see Mr Parsons and, from there, was intending to go and see Webb. Telling the young man that her husband would throw her out if he thought she had stolen the dress, she begged him to stick to the story they had agreed on.

When Webb met Banks in the street a few minutes later, Webb assured him that Mrs Banks had taken the dress by mistake. Banks asked him if he was absolutely certain and Webb said that he was. Banks then asked if Webb would mind saying so if he called on him again, to which Webb replied that he wouldn't mind.

It was obvious that the rumours of his wife's supposed theft of the dress had reached Thomas Banks's ears and that, as a prominent businessman in the town, his reputation would probably suffer as a consequence. It therefore seems as though Banks was intending to sue those responsible for spreading rumours about his wife and was sounding out Francis Webb to see if he could rely on him to support his case.

Francis Webb had one more detail to reveal to the court. Just a few days before the murder, he was asked to take some dresses round to the Banks's home. That morning, Elizabeth Banks – Thomas's sister – had been in the shop looking at dresses and Webb assumed that they were for her. He therefore delivered the box of garments to the house she shared with her mother.

It was only when Emma Banks's maid came to the shop that he realised that the dresses were intended for Emma. He collected them from Elizabeth and took them to Emma's home, where she met him on the doorstep and asked if he had told her mother-in-law where he was taking the dresses. Emma was not pleased when he told her that he had. She quickly unpacked the parcel but rejected all the dresses, which Webb took back to the shop. Webb was back at Emma's house the next morning with yet more dresses and, once again, Emma tried to persuade him to get Mr Parsons to meet her to talk about the misappropriated dress. Once again, Webb passed on the message and, once again, William Parsons refused to go.

Webb had not seen Emma Banks again until after the murder. By that time, she had gained the impression that she wasn't exactly welcomed at Parsons' shop. Webb and Mrs Banks chatted about the murder and Webb told her that 'it is quite evident there was a woman in it.' Emma said she didn't believe that but asked Webb if the police had any suspects at which Webb replied tellingly, 'If I am not greatly mistaken, it was a man with plenty of money and a very bad wife.'

Mr Lentall substantiated Francis Webb's evidence about the missing dress, although he was obviously unable to confirm or refute Webb's testimony about his series of secret meetings with Emma Banks. Milliner Sarah Ellen Ley then told the court that Mr Banks had indeed been to see Mr Parsons at the shop on 15 November.

Henry Smith testified to having seen Banks and Parsons arguing in the street on either 17 or 18 November, while James Chambers told the court that at 7.45 p.m. on 19 November he had seen Parsons apparently visiting Emma Banks, while her husband was at The Chequers Inn. If Chambers was to be believed, Parsons had spent at least fifteen minutes at the Banks's home.

John Young was next to take the stand. Thomas Banks had installed Young as a tenant landlord at The Chequers and, on the night of the murder, Young had driven three passengers to the Railway Tavern in his carriage. As he was passing the tollhouse on the Weyhill Road, he saw Emma Banks walking with solicitor Henry Loscombe towards the pub. He stopped to offer them a lift, but Emma declined.

When Young reached the tavern at about 8.55 p.m., he met Thomas Banks and asked him if he wanted a lift back to Andover. Banks walked off, saying that he would be back in a minute. Young waited for a quarter of an hour, but Banks did not return, so Young set off for Andover with another passenger, John Cowlin Stockley, a painter and glazier.

The three passengers Young had taken to the inn were the landlord's wife Martha Guyatt, her servant and a girl called Emily Bennett. Martha Guyatt was Thomas Banks's sister and, having passed the heavily pregnant Emma making her way up to the tavern, she sent her servant and Emily to intercept her to tell her that her husband was no longer there.

Emma thanked them and turned back towards Andover. This was about five minutes before Young and Stockley left the Railway Tavern to return to Andover and they fully expected to catch up with her on the road. However, they didn't see her again, even though Young, who was rather concerned for her welfare, took the carriage along an alternative route to see if she had gone that way.

On the Friday after the murder, Young had told Banks that he suspected him of killing Parsons but Banks assured him that his conscience was clear and that he could account for every moment of his time on the night of the murder. Young disputed this, reminding Banks that he had left the Railway Tavern and not returned.

Several more witnesses testified before the magistrates about Banks's presence at the Railway Tavern and the fact that he had left suddenly. Then it was left to the lawyers to make their closing arguments.

Mr Poulden, for the prosecution, admitted that all the evidence against Thomas and Emma Banks was circumstantial but reminded the court that circumstantial evidence was often the best kind as men could lie but circumstances could not. Nothing had been taken from the dead man's pockets, said Poulden, and Banks was a wealthy man and had no need of money. Mrs Banks had committed a felony in Mr Parsons' shop and, as a consequence, ill-feeling had developed between the accused and Parsons.

Defence counsel Mr Poland pointed out that there were hundreds of people going about their business near Andover who could just as easily have committed the murder. Parsons had been prepared to treat the shoplifting incident as a simple mistake and had told Banks so when he had seen him at the shop. This fact alone removed revenge or malice as a possible motive for Banks to kill Parsons. The prosecution had inferred that Parsons had gone to the cowshed for a pre-arranged immoral liaison with Emma Banks but Poland pointed out that Mrs Banks was eight months pregnant. Poland also made the point that it was Thomas Banks's habit to walk his dog every morning – would he have taken his dog so close to the scene of the murder the morning after and risked it sniffing out the body of his victim? There was, Poland insisted, no case to answer.

The magistrates disagreed and after a private debate lasting for thirty minutes, committed Thomas and Emma Banks to stand trial at the next Winchester Assizes.

Meanwhile, *The Times* bemoaned the fact that there had apparently been at least five ear-witnesses to the crime and not one of them had intervened. Was murder of as little account in Hampshire as it used to be in California, the paper asked its readers?

By the time the case came up for trial at the assizes on 1 March 1859, Emma Banks had given birth to a son, Thomas Alexander, in Winchester Prison.

Mr Baron Watson, the presiding judge, had ten cases on his list, one of which was the murder of William Parsons. After considering the facts of the case, Baron Watson recommended that the Grand Jury should dismiss the bill against the defendants, as, in his opinion, there was absolutely no case to answer. There was nothing to connect either Thomas or Emma Banks with the murder weapon and no evidence of any malice between them and the victim. The judge pointed out that should Mr and Mrs Banks be tried and acquitted then they could not be tried again, even if more evidence against them was to emerge in the future.

With the case against him dismissed, Banks returned to Andover determined to clear his name. He had already prepared a pamphlet entitled *The Mal-administration of Justice by Borough Magistrates*. Now he followed this with a second, *Justice in Andover*. In the following months, Banks was extremely vocal in his condemnation of the legal proceedings that had seen both him and his wife committed for a trial, which had, in effect, been dismissed through lack of evidence against them.

Meanwhile, in spite of the offer of a £100 reward for information leading to the arrest of the murderer of William Parsons, no such information was forthcoming and it appeared as though the case would remain unsolved.

Until, in 1892, more than thirty years after the murder, a man walked into a police station in Lancashire and confessed to the murder of William Parsons. Rowland George Lush told police that he had been with a two friends on the night in question and had caught William Parsons with another man's wife. Believing this to be wrong, the three had taken it upon themselves to chastise Parsons and had chased him with a stick, intending to hit him on the back. However, Parsons had accidentally been hit over the head and immediately fell to the ground, dead. At this, the three men ran away.

When interviewed by the police, Lush got some of the details about the murder correct and others completely wrong. He named his two companions as Thomas Banks and Frederick Guyatt, Banks's brother-in-law. However, Lush told the police that he and his companions were the same age whereas in reality, at the time of the murder, Lush would have been under twenty years old, and Banks and Guyatt in their early to mid thirties. Lush also said that the murder weapon was a stake that was pulled from the hedge rather than a heavy branch that had been specially cut for the purpose.

Lush was remanded in Strangeways Prison while the Chief Constable of Hampshire made some investigations into the validity of his statements. When Lush was finally brought before magistrates on 12 March 1892, charged with the wilful murder of William Parsons, the Chief Constable wrote saying that he could find no evidence to substantiate the prisoner's confession. This left the court with no other option than to discharge him since, without any evidence to support his account, his confession to the murder meant nothing.

The phenomenon of the false confession to crimes is, of course, well known but even so, it seems strange that Lush should suddenly feel the need to confess to a murder that happened more than thirty years previously. A family man, he had no criminal record at the time of his confession and no history of mental illness and, according to contemporary accounts, seemed completely sober. Was Lush guilty and, if so, had the crime played on his mind and troubled his conscience to the extent that he could no longer bear the burden of his guilt? Or was he, as was widely assumed at the time, simply a hoaxer? Either way, it seems strange that, in recounting the murder, he should name Thomas Banks and his brother-in-law as his companions and even more strange that, in his memory, both men were the same age as he was at the time when in actuality, both would have been more than ten years older.

Yet, relying on contemporary newspaper accounts of the murder, there seem to be several more anomalies in the case.

For a start, the murder weapon was described as being 'thicker than a man's wrist'. The choice of a stout stick as the murder weapon seems strange in that a length of wood of that thickness would have taken some time to cut, especially as it was cut twice to remove the top and the smaller side branches were also removed. This suggests a degree of premeditation to the murder and begs the question why the killer or killers didn't just use a knife. One possible explanation is that whoever attacked Parsons didn't actually intend to kill him but just to give him a beating.

The fact that more than £3 was found in Parsons' pocket after his death seems to rule out robbery as a motive for his killing, unless the killer had intended simply to knock Parsons out and rob him and, having realised that he had hit him too hard and his victim was dead, panicked and fled before searching him. Yet, if robbery was not the motive then it seems likely that Parsons was killed by someone who had a personal grudge against him.

Why was Parsons in the field in the first place? Was he expecting to meet someone at the cowshed or had he been lured there by his killer? Given that Parsons had told his wife that he was just popping out to post a letter, a pre-arranged assignation with a woman seems the most probable scenario. Knowing how anxious Emma Banks was that her husband and his family would find out about the stolen dress, could he have been blackmailing her and expecting certain favours, sexual or otherwise, in exchange for corroborating her story that the theft was simply a mistake? If this was the case, then Thomas Banks seems to be the most probable candidate for the murderer. But then again, if Banks did kill Parsons, why was he so publicly vocal about what he considered to be the ineptitude of the legal system after the case against him was dismissed? If Banks were guilty then he ran the risk of facing a trial in future, if and when new evidence emerged. Wouldn't a guilty man have been more likely to fade quietly into the background rather than continue to keep the case at the forefront of everyone's mind by publishing pamphlets and making public speeches?

Finally, what drove a seemingly sane, respectable man like George Lush to confess to the murder after more than thirty years? If Lush is to be believed, then his companions that night were Thomas Banks and Frederick Guyatt. Could Fredrick's wife, Martha, have been the woman that Parsons was expecting to meet in the cowshed? It should be noted that no shred of evidence was ever produced to suggest that William Parsons was enjoying extra-marital affairs with Emma Banks, Martha Guyatt or indeed any other woman, even though he seemed to have a reputation in Andover as something of a ladies man. If this reputation was deserved, was his killer a jealous husband or boyfriend?

There are so many questions about the death of William Parsons that remain unanswered and the identity of his killer or killers remains a mystery, his murder unsolved to this day.

8

'IF YOU FORGET TO BE A SON, I SHALL FORGET TO BE A FATHER'

Gosport, 1860

In March 1860, Michael Hynes, a sergeant in the 10th Foot Regiment, was on furlough from his posting at Aldershot and staying with his father-in-law at his home in Gosport. On 9 March, the fifth day of his holiday, he spent much of afternoon drinking, rolling home at seven o'clock in the evening decidedly the worse for wear.

His wife and parents-in-law pressed him to stay at home and have his tea but Hynes was determined to enjoy his leave as fully as possible and insisted on going out drinking again. Concerned for Michael's safety, his father-in-law John Clarke thought it prudent to accompany him and the two men went to The Rummer public house in Gosport, where they met up with a man named Brown. Brown drank a few pints of beer with them before leaving and, once he had gone, Hynes and Clarke each drank two glasses of gin. Hynes ended his drinking spree with a large whisky, by which time he was completely inebriated and needed to be escorted home by his father-in-law.

Once there, his mother-in-law asked him once again to sit down and eat his tea, reminding him that her brother was coming to spend an evening with the family. Her simple request seemed to send Hynes into a paroxysm of rage.

'Am I to be controlled in this way?' he roared, giving Mrs Clarke a hefty push that sent her sprawling into a chair.

Mrs Clarke remonstrated with him, struggling to her feet, at which Hynes gave her another shove that sent her flying. By now, John Clarke had seen enough.

'If you forget to be a son, I shall forget to be a father,' he warned Hynes.

Clarke's words were like a red bag to a bull. Soon Hynes was like a madman, physically fighting both Mr and Mrs Clarke and, no matter how hard John Clarke tried, he was unable to subdue his much younger son-in-law. Eventually, since Clarke's presence seemed to be angering Hynes even more, Mrs Clarke sent him out of the house and John Clarke seized the opportunity to run for a policeman.

The noise of the pitched battle and the cries of 'Murder!' from the house in Chapman's Yard soon attracted the attention of the Clarkes' next-door neighbour, Mrs Ann Shein, who bravely came in to see if she could help. By now, Hynes had taken his sword from its place on the sitting room wall, although he hadn't yet drawn it from its scabbard. Sixty-four-year-old Mrs Shein tried to pacify Michael Hynes, without success. Instead, he turned his violent anger on her, pushing Mrs Clarke out of the house and locking the door behind him.

Sixteen-year-old Sarah Clarke had been upstairs when the fight broke out. Now she came downstairs to see Mrs Shein sitting in a chair and her brother-in-law standing nearby with his sword drawn. Terrified, Sarah ran back upstairs and jumped out of the bedroom window.

Concerned for Mrs Shein's safety, Mrs Clarke called for her son, David, who managed to force the locked door open. As soon as he did so, Hynes rushed at them waving his drawn sword and Mrs Clarke and David Shein ran for their lives. When John Clarke returned, having been unable to find a policeman, Hynes was charging about the yard, flourishing his sword. Clarke picked up a poker and tried to disarm him.

With Hynes occupied in the yard, Mrs Clarke and David Shein rushed into the house along with another neighbour, David Hutchins. Finding Mrs Shein lying unconscious on the floor with a head wound, her son and the neighbour quickly removed her to her own house, while Mrs Clarke rounded up several children from the house and shepherded them to safety in a neighbour's home, locking the house behind her.

The commotion soon attracted the attention of PC Young, who was patrolling his beat in Gosport High Street. He went to investigate the disturbance, finding Michael Hynes charging up the passage between the houses, his sword drawn, threatening to run the police officer through. Young went for reinforcements and Hynes was later overpowered and arrested.

A doctor had been called to attend to Mrs Shein and found that she had three cuts on her forehead, all of which were between three and four inches long. Mrs Shein's skull was fractured beneath all three of the cuts, with what Mr Wharton, the surgeon, termed as 'compound cominuted fractures' – in other words, the bones were completely splintered and fragments were protruding through her skin. In addition to her head wounds, Mrs Shein had a cut beneath her left eye, two inch-long cuts on her left arm and severe contusions on her right. The surgeon removed several fragments of bone from Mrs Shein's head.

Hynes' coat, waistcoat, scabbard and sword belt were found in the house, heavily spotted with blood, as was his sword. With so many eyewitnesses, it was a simple matter for the police to arrest the perpetrator of the vicious attack on Mrs Shein and Michael Hynes was detained in Winchester Prison, charged with cutting and wounding with attempt to murder.

Church parade in Wellington Avenue, Aldershot. (Author's collection)

Although Wharton's prognosis for Mrs Shein's survival was initially good, she was by no means out of danger and was too ill to give evidence when Hynes appeared before magistrates on 17 March. Hynes could remember very little of the events of the evening of 9 March and was completely devastated on being told what had happened. Normally a steady and sober man, he was an exemplary soldier and was on the verge of promotion to quartermaster at the time of the attack on Mrs Shein.

In May 1860, while Hynes was awaiting his trial in Winchester Prison, Mrs Shein lost her long fight for life. She had developed inflammation of the brain, followed by an abscess, which led to her first becoming completely paralysed, then her eventual death.

Thus, when Hynes stood trial at the Winchester Assizes on 16 July 1860, it was on a charge of wilful murder. The trial was presided over by Mr Justice Keating, with Mr Poulden and Mr Bentham prosecuting and Mr W.M. Cooke defending.

The prosecution called a number of witnesses to the events of 9 March, including Mr and Mrs Clarke, their daughter Sarah, David Shein, David Hutchins and Mr Wharton as well as several neighbours, who had seen Hynes through the windows, hacking at something on the floor with his sword. The prosecution rested in the belief that they had proved beyond all reasonable doubt that Hynes had wilfully murdered Mrs Shein.

Mr Cooke then spoke for the prisoner, telling the jury that there was absolutely no malice in Hynes' mind at the time of the attack on Mrs Shein and that he was in such a state of 'mad excitement' that the offence amounted to manslaughter, not murder. Cooke called several officers from Hynes' regiment, all of whom gave him an excellent character reference.

It was then left to Mr Justice Keating to sum up. Keating told the jury that it was a certainty that Mrs Shein's death had been as a result of the attack on her by the defendant, which, by English law, was murder. It was not necessary for any malice aforethought to have been shown by Hynes towards the victim.

Keating warned the jury not to be swayed by compassion in view of the previous good character of the defendant – if the jury believed that the death of Mrs Shein was caused by the deadly weapon used by the prisoner, even if he was intoxicated, there was nothing to warrant a reduction of the charge from murder to manslaughter. Thus, if the jury believed the evidence they had heard in court, a verdict of 'Guilty of wilful murder' was the only option open to them.

The jury deliberated for some time before returning to court to announce that they had no chance of reaching a consensus since some of the members were still in doubt about the question of malice.

Mr Justice Keating embarked on a lengthy explanation of the legal term malice. It could, he stated, either refer to a feeling expressed towards an individual or, in law, it could be the inference from an act done. In other words, if the use of a deadly weapon was likely to cause harmful effects, the law inferred malice.

He used the example of a man firing a gun into a crowd to illustrate his explanation. The man might not know any individual amongst the crowd but, if death ensued, in the eyes of the law, he would still be exhibiting malice, since he would be well aware of the potential outcome of his actions. Keating reiterated that the defendant's intoxication at the time of the murder could not be seen as a mitigating circumstance and that there was no provocation, hence nothing about the case warranted a reduction of the charge from murder to manslaughter.

The jury consulted for a few minutes before asking if the medical witnesses might be recalled as they wished to be absolutely certain that Mrs Shein's head injuries had been the cause of her death. The judge read through the medical evidence and assured the jury that her wounds had caused the abscess on the brain that killed her. Yet the jury were adamant – they wanted to hear the words directly from the mouths of the doctors.

The judge patiently recalled the medical witnesses, who testified as one that Mrs Shein died as a result of the injuries inflicted on her by Michael Hynes. One of the jurors remarked that the interval between the wounds and Mrs Shein's death seemed too long, at which the doctors assured him that time had nothing to do with the matter.

'If she had been a younger woman, would she have recovered?' asked another juror.

Keating was losing patience. 'Gentlemen, has a person a right to take away a woman's life because she is old?' he asked, testily.

'My Lord, may we not give a verdict of manslaughter?' queried the juror.

Once again, Keating stressed that there was absolutely nothing about the case that warranted such a verdict and, when the juror tried to argue the point, he dismissed the jury and told them to go and consider their verdict. 'You can give what verdict you please' he told them. 'You are to decide on the evidence and give your verdict on the responsibility of your oaths. It is the evidence you are sworn to act on. You have the power of disbelieving every witness called. You may think the whole is a fiction, but you do so on your own responsibility – that of your oaths.'

Four hours later, the jury sent in a written question, asking the judge whether manslaughter supposed an accidental killing. Keating was, by this time, almost apoplectic. He sent for the jury and told them that he couldn't understand their question. Manslaughter could be a killing by accident, if the person was involved in the commission of an illegal act, not amounting to a felony, and accidentally killed another person. If a man was engaged in a sudden quarrel with another man and the two fought, the one not intending to kill the other but unfortunately doing so, that would be manslaughter. But, according to the law, the offence of manslaughter only existed when a person killed another after provocation. In this case, there was no provocation and, in the absence of any provocation, the prisoner had used a deadly weapon, which resulted in the death of a woman.

The jury now informed the judge that, with the exception of one member, they had agreed on their verdict.

'You must endeavour to convince him by reason' the judge instructed, telling them to look at the facts of the case and not trouble themselves with questions of law.

After a few minutes more deliberation, the jury finally delivered their verdict. They found Michael Hynes 'Guilty of the wilful murder of Ann Shein', although they gave a strong recommendation for mercy for the prisoner on account of his previous good behaviour. Keating passed sentence of death of Hynes, who immediately collapsed in the dock and had to be supported by two warders.

As the final preparations were made at Winchester Prison for his execution, Hynes drew great comfort from his Roman Catholic faith. However, shortly before he was due to hang, it was announced that Hynes had been reprieved.

Note: In some contemporary accounts of the murder, Hynes is alternatively named Michael Haines and Mr and Mrs Clarke's name is also spelled Clark. I have taken the most frequently used name and spellings for this account.

9

'WHAT HARM HAVE I EVER DONE YOU?'

Aldershot, 1861

The West Block Permanent Barracks at Aldershot were home to the 78th Highlanders, who were regarded as a highly disciplined regiment of soldiers. However, on Saturday, 23 November 1861, there was a woeful lapse in the regiment's hitherto exemplary behaviour, which ultimately led to the death of two of its number.

At a few minutes past 8 p.m., Sergeant John Dickson and Corporal Campbell were performing the nightly roll call. They had reached room number 11 and were shouting out the names of the occupants when one of the soldiers picked up a rifle, aimed it at Sergeant Dickson's back and fired. Even as the deafening sound of the shot rang out in the confined barracks, Private Thomas Jackson turned and calmly replaced the rifle on the rack.

Dickson turned slowly to face the room. 'Who did that?' he asked.

'I did it, old boy,' replied Jackson.

'What harm have I ever done you?' asked Sergeant Dickson, before collapsing to the ground. Meanwhile, Corporal Campbell, who had been standing next to Dickson, said that he too was shot and abruptly left the room.

Private William Marshall seized Jackson's arm and, with the help of five other soldiers, escorted him down to the guard room where he was handed over to the sergeant of the guard. There was another prisoner already in the guard room who was drunk and Jackson was briefly locked in with him while the sergeant went to find some handcuffs. When the door was opened again, Jackson was attacking the other prisoner, almost strangling him. 'It's a pity I did not get more of you ******* shot', was Jackson's only comment.

Meanwhile, Joseph Jee, the 78th Highlanders' surgeon had been called urgently from the mess to attend to the two injured soldiers. On reaching room 11, Jee found that thirty-five-year-old Dickson was beyond his help. The ball from the rifle had entered his chest about an inch below his shoulder, fracturing one of his ribs and passing through his lungs and the base of his heart before exiting through his back. The same ball had then struck Campbell on the right shoulder, shattering the head and neck of his humerus bone. Although the Corporal had survived, his injuries were serious and required an operation.

The civilian police were sent for and Superintendent William Howard arrested Jackson, charging him with the murder of John Dickson. Jackson made no reply.

Municipal Gardens, Aldershot, 1915. (Author's collection)

'Do you understand it?' asked Howard.

'I understand, sure – where's the difference to me?' said Jackson. On his way to the police station Jackson told Howard, 'I know my destiny. I know what I've got to suffer. The ******* gave me six months' hard labour once and now I've given him twelve.'

Nineteen-year-old Thomas Jackson from Barnard Castle, near Durham, had joined the regiment in June 1858 by special authority, since he was underage at the time. He had deserted only two months later and had joined another regiment under an assumed name. Returned to the 78th Regiment in 1860, he was hardly a model soldier and had only recently been released from prison after serving a six-month sentence for breaking his rifle and a window. On his release from prison, Jackson had been demoted to the level of recruit and, as such, was not permitted to have ammunition. However, Private Munro, who slept in the adjacent bed to Jackson's, had been allowed ammunition and Jackson had stolen one round from Munro's ammunition pouch, which hung at the head of his cot, and loaded it into his own rifle.

On 25 November, the deputy coroner for Hampshire, Mr T. Pain, opened an inquest into the death of Sergeant Dickson at the Tilbury's Royal Hotel. Brought from the police station, where he had been confined in the cells since his arrest, Thomas Jackson maintained an air of cool indifference as he listened to the testimony of his room mates, who all gave almost identical accounts of the events leading up to Dickson's death.

Duncan Anderson, William Marshall and Andrew Cormick had all seen more or less the same thing. As the two officers stood taking roll call, Jackson had suddenly snatched a rifle from the rack, put it into the 'ready' position and fired a single shot into the back of Sergeant Dickson, who was standing only six feet in front of him. Most of the witnesses had heard Jackson making threats towards the sergeant in the past and Anderson stated that Jackson had frequently said that he would be hung for Dickson. Marshall told the inquest that, as he was escorting Jackson down to the guard room, Jackson had told him that he had intended to load all the rifles he could lay his hands on and discharge them at the regiment during parade. He had also threatened another officer, Sergeant Profitt, saying that it would be his turn next and that he would be killed by 15 December. When the coroner questioned Sergeant-Major John Pocock, he revealed that a soldier who had been in prison with Jackson was scheduled for release on 15 December – he had been imprisoned for threatening to kill Sergeant Profitt.

Having heard from surgeon Joseph Jee, the coroner asked Thomas Jackson if he wished to say anything. 'No, I don't wish to say anything. I've got nothing to say,' responded Jackson.

The inquest jury returned a verdict of wilful murder against Thomas Jackson, afterwards expressing their concern about the frequency of such incidents and suggesting that the government should be forced to act to make access to ammunition more difficult. Mr Pain told them that, only twelve months previously, he had conducted an inquest on another similar case, when a sergeant and a corporal had been shot by a soldier and that the jury then had made a similar recommendation. As a result, he had written to His Royal Highness, the Commander-in-Chief, suggesting that soldiers were not allowed ready access to ammunition. Although he had received an acknowledgment to his letter, Mr Pain bemoaned the fact that, in the past year alone, there had been similar cases at Preston, Plymouth and Colchester, not to mention numerous suicides by soldiers. Pain suggested that, as there was normally a non-commissioned officer in each barrack room, it seemed a simple and effectual solution to the problem to place all ammunition in his charge. He urged the jury to make their feelings known through the medium of the press.

The inquest concluded with the jury suggesting that some provision should be made for Sergeant Dickson's widow, who was currently pregnant with the couple's second child. They donated their fees as the start of a public fund for her benefit.

Thomas Jackson was brought for trial at Winchester on 13 December. His case was prosecuted by Mr H.T. Cole and Mr C. Russell and, although the judge asked a representative to act for Thomas Jackson, after pleading 'Not Guilty', he declined the assistance of counsel.

The evidence presented was a repeat of that brought before the inquest, with Jackson again refusing to make any comment. The jury retired only briefly before returning a 'Guilty' verdict and Jackson was sentenced to death. He accepted the verdict and sentence without flinching, leaving the dock with what the newspapers of the time described as 'a quick step and a jaunty air.'

After the trial, the inhabitants of Winchester petitioned the Home Secretary to get Jackson's execution carried out at the army camp, rather than at Winchester Gaol, feeling that this would act as a deterrent to any other soldiers who might be contemplating a similar act. The petition was not acted upon and on 27 December 1861, Thomas Jackson faced hangman William Calcraft at Winchester. In the run up to his execution, the condemned man had persistently refused the attentions of the prison chaplain and, as he walked briskly towards the drop, Jackson seemed to be the only person present unmoved by the occasion of his death.

Note: The victim's name is spelled both Dickson and Dixon in the contemporary newspaper reports of the case – I have taken the most frequently used version. The name of the soldier whose ammunition was taken is alternatively spelled Munro, Munroe and Monroe. There is also some discrepancy concerning one of the soldiers present in Room 11 on the night of the murder, whose name is variously given as Andrew Cormick and Henry Cormack.

10

'I THINK HE IS CRACKED, FRED'

Shirley, near Southampton, 1864

Frederick Colborne and Caroline Sophia Wing were childhood sweethearts. Frederick was employed by Southampton plumber and painter Mr Powell (also the proprietor of the Shirley Hotel), while Caroline was in service to a Mrs Burrows in Shirley. Since the couple were keen to marry, Caroline decided to move to a more highly paid job and took a position at Alresford, as a lady's maid in the household of Mr Onslow, the MP for Guildford.

The butler there was George Broomfield, a forty-seven-year-old married man who, in spite of being in service, was quite wealthy. He was known for being extremely careful with his salary and had also been left a legacy by a former employer, which afforded him an annuity of £20 a year. Broomfield took an instant shine to the new maid and, before long, began to try and force his attentions on her. Twenty-two-year-old Caroline told him repeatedly that she was already spoken for and that, even if she weren't, the difference in their ages was too great for her to ever consider a romance between them. However, Broomfield was nothing if not persistent and eventually Caroline felt that she had no other alternative but to resign her position to escape his unwanted advances.

Caroline returned to her mother's house in Shirley shortly after Christmas of 1863 and Broomfield wrote to her two or three times until she told him in no uncertain terms that his correspondence was not welcome. Soon afterwards, Broomfield came to visit her at her mother's, staying for about an hour. At the time, Caroline and Frederick had fallen out, although they soon made up their differences and Caroline later told Frederick that Broomfield had visited her specifically to propose marriage, an offer which she declined.

Finally, the message that Caroline wasn't in the slightest bit interested in him seemed to get through to Broomfield and, after he left Shirley to return to Alresford, she heard nothing more from him. On 8 May 1864, she married Frederick and the couple set up home in Union Street, Shirley.

On 3 December 1864, Fred went to collect his wages from his employer and was told that a stranger had been there, enquiring after Caroline. Mr Powell described the man to Fred, who immediately recognised the man as George Broomfield. He hurried home to find Broomfield seated at the table in the back room of the house and Caroline standing by the fireplace, looking uneasy.

High Street, Shirley, 1905. (Author's collection)

Once Broomfield and Fred had been introduced, Broomfield said laughingly, 'Well, Sir, there has been a little altercation between Carry and me.'

Fred politely told him to forget it, saying that it was all in the past and that they should let the matter drop. Broomfield then explained that he had come to tell Caroline that he was going to America.

Broomfield appeared perfectly amicable and Fred hospitably invited him to dine with them, suggesting that Caroline should fry a piece of fish.

'We must go up and pay our rent tonight,' she prompted her husband, almost as if she were trying to find an excuse to get rid of the visitor. Fred immediately offered to do it while she cooked a meal, at which Broomfield asked if he would mind booking him a room at a nearby pub while he was out.

Fred paid the rent and booked a room at the White Hart, returning home after an absence of about fifteen minutes. When he got back, Broomfield was sitting in a chair near the fire and Caroline was sitting at the table by the window, writing something.

'Mr Broomfield would like a little brandy,' she told Fred, who obligingly went out to the Shirley Hotel to fetch him some. On his return, the three ate their fish and drank a cup of tea before the two men sat down together to smoke their pipes. Caroline's mother popped in for a few minutes and then Caroline reminded Fred that they usually did their grocery shopping together on Saturday and suggested that they needed to go out and buy some provisions. Fred offered to do the shopping himself, if Caroline would write him a list, at which Broomfield suggested that Caroline went and bought the groceries, while he and Fred smoked their pipes.

By now, Caroline was anxious to get rid of Broomfield and insisted that she and Fred went out to do the shopping together. They left the house with Caroline's mother, leaving their guest alone, smoking his pipe and sipping brandy. As soon as they were safely out of earshot, Caroline turned to her husband and said, 'He says he is going to die for me, Fred.' A few minutes later, Caroline told him, 'I think he is cracked, Fred. I don't like his manner at all.'

When they returned from the shopping trip, George Broomfield was still sitting comfortably in the back room. Caroline quickly realised that they had forgotten to buy any potatoes and the ever obliging Fred offered to run out and get some.

'Don't be long, Fred,' Caroline begged him. 'I should like him gone as soon as we can.'

Fred was away for little more than ten minutes but returned to a scene of pandemonium in Union Street. As soon as they spotted Fred, his neighbours ran up to him and tried to talk to him but Fred could only think of Caroline. He elbowed aside the people who were trying to restrain him and ran into his house. As he approached the back door, he saw Caroline lying in the yard just outside, being cradled in the arms of a neighbour, Mrs Harris, blood pumping from a wound in her chest. George Broomfield lay nearby, apparently mortally wounded.

Beside himself with grief and rage, Fred Colborne seized Broomfield by the throat and had to be pulled away by neighbours before he tore him limb from limb. The police and a doctor had already been summoned and Dr Philip King Weston arrived within minutes. He could do little more for Caroline Colborne than pronounce life extinct, so he turned his attention to George Broomfield who, although seriously injured, was still conscious and able to talk.

After having been given a sip of brandy, Broomfield told the doctor that he had come to Shirley intending to settle what property he had on Caroline Colborne before leaving for America, where he intended to join the Federal Army. He told the doctor that he then planned to desert to the Confederates but that he would first join the Federals to ensure that he could get into America. 'I did it for love,' he stated, adding that, when he came to Southampton, he had no intention of shooting Caroline, saying, 'What I have suffered, no one knows.'

Several letters were found in his pocket, one of which he appeared to have dictated to Caroline, since it was written in her handwriting and topped with a brief note saying that he had asked Mrs Colborne to write it for him as he felt too ill to do so himself. The letter was addressed to his wife and opened: 'My dear, dear Ann, These are the last words you will ever hear from me. I feel I have broken your heart.' The letter went on to outline Broomfield's plans to go to America, then continued:

Oh, my darling Ann, I shall not have your kind and affectionate eyes and [illegible] to watch over me as you ever have done, particularly the last nine months, night and day. Had I never gone to Alresford, my happy home never would have been broken up.

The letter ended with details of Broomfield's estate and an instruction to a neighbour: 'Dear Sarah, render all the assistance you can to my dear wife; tell her not to fret about me; I am not worthy of her doing so. Goodbye.'

A second letter was addressed to Fred Colborne and written in a tremulous hand. The writer asked Fred to forgive him and entertained hopes that they would all meet again in heaven, along with Broomfield's wife, Ann. Broomfield asked Fred to 'talagraph' a Mr Brown, to let him know that he was dead and begged to be buried with Carry.

Broomfield was rushed to the Royal South Hants Infirmary at Southampton, suffering from a gun shot wound to his chest that was so severe that he was not expected to survive. His wife, Ann, rushed to his bedside from her home in Islington. Still fully conscious on his arrival at hospital, he told the house surgeon that, some years ago, he had been shot in the head, since when he suffered from fits of mental derangement. He also told the police officers at his bedside that he had asked Caroline to go to America with him and, when she refused, told her, 'Then we must die together.' At that, he pulled out a pistol and shot her once in the chest, before turning the gun on himself. Somehow, his first shot bounced harmlessly off his chest but the second passed through his chest beneath his lungs. 'I am guilty of shooting Caroline Sophia Colborne on Saturday 3 December, but I was not at this time in a sound state of mind,' was his final statement to the police.

An inquest was opened into the death of Caroline Colborne at the Shirley Hotel by Hampshire coroner Mr J.H. Todd. With Broomfield still gravely ill in hospital, the inquest heard from surgeon Mr Weston who, with the assistance of Mr William Mott, had conducted a post-mortem examination on the body of Caroline Colborne. For the first time, it was revealed to the general public that she had been in her seventh or eighth month of pregnancy. A ball from a pistol had passed between the first and second ribs on the left-hand side of her chest, piercing her heart and the lower part of her right lung before hitting her fifth rib on the right side of her chest. This deflected the ball, which eventually finished up lodged beneath her shoulder blade and, according to both surgeons, death would have been instantaneous.

In addition to the surgeons, Frederick Colborne and several of the Colborne's neighbours, Mrs Ann Broomfield was called to give evidence at the inquest. She stated that her husband had lived with her at Islington since January that year, having left his position at Alresford due to nervous illness. For the past nine months, he had been in such a state with his nerves that she had been afraid to leave him alone but, on 3 December, he had been 'as mad as a March hare' and she had been unable to keep him indoors. He left home at about midday, telling his wife that he would be home in a few hours and the next she heard of him was a telegram from the Southampton police.

Questioned by the coroner, Mrs Broomfield said that she had been married for about six years. On his return from Alresford, George had told her that he would not deceive her and that he had formed an attachment with Miss Wing but that it was all off now. Since then, he had never spoken of her again. She knew nothing of his plans to go to America and told the inquest that, when he left home on 3 December, as far as she was aware, her husband did not have a gun. Her husband now appeared sincerely penitent and told her that he must have been mad when he shot Caroline.

The coroner's jury returned a verdict of wilful murder against George Broomfield, and the coroner charged him to appear at the next Winchester Assizes, although with little hope that he would live to do so.

However, against all odds, George Broomfield pulled through and, by mid-January 1865, he was considered well enough to appear before magistrates. Since he was still in hospital, the magistrates held a special sitting there, at which Broomfield was constantly attended by his wife and a house surgeon, Dr Short. He was reported as 'having a deathly pale countenance' and, at times, did not appear to understand what was going on, asking more than once, 'Where are we now?' Asked if he wanted to make any statement, Broomfield replied, 'No. I can only say I am a dying man – a dying man.'

Broad Street, Alresford. (Author's collection)

Nevertheless, Broomfield survived to appear before Mr Justice Keating at the next Hampshire Assizes held at Winchester on 16 July 1865. His case was prosecuted by Mr Bere and Mr Compton, while Broomfield was defended by Mr Coleridge QC and Mr H.T. Cole.

In the dock, Broomfield appeared so weak that, before commencing the proceedings, the judge sent for the surgeon at Winchester Prison, seeking reassurance that the prisoner was actually fit to stand trial. When the surgeon determined that he was, the judge asked Broomfield whether he pleaded guilty or not guilty to the charge of wilful murder against him. 'I wish to die' was Broomfield's only response, which Keating recorded as a plea of 'Not Guilty'.

The prosecution maintained that Broomfield was strongly, if wrongly, in love with Caroline Colborne at the time of her murder. He wanted her for himself and, if he could not have her, could not bear to think of her being with another man.

For the defence, the case was less clear-cut. Mr Coleridge addressed the court on behalf of his client, admitting that the prosecution was correct in contending that Caroline had met her death at the hands of George Broomfield. There was nothing about the case that would warrant a reduction of the charge from murder to manslaughter – no provocation, no quarrel and no mistake. Normally, a person who committed a cruel murder and shed man's blood must die because he had broken God's commandments and violated the laws of man. However, in this case it had pleased God to so disturb Broomfield's reason and so ruin his mind that he had done neither of these things, in the sense that he was not legally and properly responsible for his act. His hand was the hand that fired the pistol but, at the time, his mind was absent from the act, which was the irresistible consequence of some disease of the mind. In cases such as this, the law acquitted him and it would be up to the jury to follow the directives of the law.

Coleridge then detailed Broomfield's life prior to the murder for the court. He had been in service to the Delap family until the death of Colonel Delap, after which his devoted service to the colonel's widow was such that the family rewarded him with an annuity. An unwise investment had caused the loss of hundreds of pounds of his inheritance, which was personally devastating to a man of nervous disposition. Yet he was so highly regarded by the Delap family that they made up the loss of his money.

He married his wife, Ann, in 1859. Like him, she had been in service and was an older woman. The couple had lived very affectionately together but, in 1860, he had been present with his employer, Mr Onslow MP, at a shooting party on the estate of Lord George Beauclerk, where he was accidentally shot in the head.

More than thirty pieces of shot were extracted from his head and back but many more remained and, from that moment on, he was a changed man. He imagined that he was suffering from a number of diseases and his hypochondria had reduced him to the miserable wreck of a man that the court saw before them now.

In 1863, while Broomfield was back in the service of Miss Delap, Miss Onslow came to stay, accompanied by her maid, Caroline Wing. Finding himself 'in love' with Caroline, Broomfield handed in his notice to Miss Delap. He later retracted it but, by then, his mind had become so impaired that Miss Delap thought it best to let him go. He then returned to work for the Onslow family, where he remained until January 1864, when he was forced to give up work due to his ill health.

From that time, he had been prey to a number of delusions, the most prominent of which was that both he and his wife were seriously ill and dying. Numerous times, he requested the services of his doctor, Dr Tweed, who could find nothing wrong with either of them apart from the fact that Broomfield was a hypochondriac and suffering from a disease of the mind. It was Tweed's opinion that Broomfield's condition was worsening and that, although he posed no danger to anybody else, there was a strong likelihood that he would commit suicide. Tweed had prescribed a change of air and bed rest for his patient and, by 3 December 1864, Broomfield had been in bed for some time.

He escaped from his wife on the pretext of gong out to buy a newspaper and, once out of the house, he visited several tradesmen to try and borrow some money. Having successfully obtained £10, he visited Oxford Street, where he purchased a pistol.

Broomfield was a gentle, affectionate man and his actions in shooting Caroline Colborne were totally inconsistent and out of character. Coleridge then called a number of witnesses to support his arguments.

All testified that Broomfield was a man of the highest moral and religious character but that, after he was shot, his mind had 'gone'. He frequently cried and refused to eat, telling people that his head was empty or that his stomach was falling to pieces. He had been wracked by delusions that his wife was seriously ill and dying, which had broken his heart.

Mr Brown, who had lent him £10, with which he then purchased the weapon used to kill Caroline Colborne, told the court that, having given Broomfield the money, he looked more closely at him and saw that he looked wild and his eyes were staring out of his head. Brown then had a change of heart about lending him the money and tried to detain him but Broomfield had managed to escape. Brown was convinced that, at the time, Broomfield was quite mad.

Dr Tweed told the court that, apart from a touch of indigestion, Broomfield's only medical problems were in his mind. He complained that his blood was turning to water and that there was something trickling from his heart. His chronic hypochondria convinced him that both he and his wife were about to die and his apprehension of death caused him a great lowness of spirit. Tweed had given him medicine merely to placate him and advised frequent changes of scene and bed rest. In Tweed's opinion, Broomfield's mind was 'off balance' and he was at grave risk of committing suicide, although at no time had the doctor believed him to be a danger to other people.

In his summary of the evidence for the jury, Mr Justice Keating told them that the prosecution had proved beyond reasonable doubt that Caroline Colborne had died at Broomfield's hands. Thus, it was for the jury to decide whether or not they believed that Broomfield had been insane at the time of the murder. Having explained in great detail the legal definitions of insanity, the judge dismissed the jury to begin their deliberations.

Much to the surprise of everyone in the court, the jury returned a verdict of 'Guilty' adding no rider to their verdict that the accused was insane at the time. This left the judge with no alternative and sentence of death was passed on Broomfield, who happily accepted his fate, having already expressed a wish to die.

However, his wish was not to be granted. Examined by doctors after his trial, he was judged to be of unsound mind and was reprieved and sent to Millbank Prison. In July 1866, an application was made to transfer him to Broadmoor Criminal Lunatic Asylum and, by November 1877, doctors at Broadmoor considered him to have improved sufficiently to sanction his discharge, providing some competent person were found to supervise him. In spite of questions being asked in parliament, after consideration of the application for his release, the Secretary of State authorised his release.

11

'OH, MOTHER,
MY POOR MOTHER'

Portsea, 1865

At six o'clock on the morning of 5 June 1865, residents of Montague Street in Landport, Portsea, awoke to see a distressed child standing shivering in the doorway of a house. The little girl, who was about five years old, was completely naked and when next-door neighbour Mrs Harris went to comfort her, all the sobbing child could say was, 'Oh, mother, my poor mother.'

Since there was no sign of Maria Clements, the child's mother, Mrs Harris went into the house to check on her whereabouts. The cause of the child's anguish immediately became obvious – Maria Clements lay stiff and cold on her back on the floor of a downstairs room. Her clothing was in a state of disarray, her dress torn and her skirts pulled above her waist. She wore no shoes or stockings.

Mrs Harris ushered the frightened little girl and her younger sister out of the house before summoning a doctor and the police. When surgeon Mr Bentham arrived, he examined the woman and noted no marks of violence on her body other than several obvious bites on her cheeks, chin and neck. He estimated that Maria Clements had been dead for around eight hours and, at a later post-mortem examination, conducted by Bentham and a colleague, Mr Gould, it was discovered that she had been bitten on her windpipe with sufficient force to prevent her from breathing and so suffocate her.

Maria Clements had obviously been brutally murdered and, in such cases, the prime suspect is usually the husband. However, Maria had been married for fourteen years to a ship's stoker, and when the police opened their enquiries, they were quickly able to establish beyond any doubt that Charles Clements had spent the previous night on board his ship, HMS *Diadem*, which was docked in Portsmouth harbour. At that stage, the only possible witnesses to the murder were two very frightened and distressed little girls, both of whom were under five years old. The police questioned both children but could only determine that the older girl had heard a scream in the middle of the night but had not got up to investigate its source.

When the murder was publicised in the local newspapers, the landlord of the nearby Queen's Head pub in Greatham Street came forward to tell the police that Maria Clements had been drinking in his premises on the afternoon and evening of 4 June. According to Mr Wyatt, she was accompanied by her two children and, having ordered a pint of beer, struck up a conversation with a group of three soldiers, who the landlord identified as Privates Hughes, Parker and O'Neil. She seemed to get on particularly well with John Hughes, who apparently came from the same town in Ireland as Maria Clements. Hughes and Maria chatted for some time, while Hughes amused the two children by bouncing them on his knee and putting his cap on the youngest girl's head.

Several quarts of beer were bought and drunk by the party before it came time for the soldiers to leave and return to barracks. Hughes tried to persuade Maria Clements to go home but she was reluctant to do so and although his two companions urged him to leave her and come back with them, he insisted that he should first see Maria and her children safely home.

Maria was equally determined to stay in the pub and eventually Hughes picked up the youngest child and, taking the oldest child by the hand, he took them to their house, expecting their mother to follow. When she didn't, he left the children on their doorstep and went back to the pub to try and persuade Maria to come home. Maria was still intent on staying where she was, leaving Hughes no choice but to collect the children from their home and return them to their mother.

At this point, landlord Mr Wyatt asked him, 'What have you to do with the woman? She is a married woman.' Hughes insisted that Maria was a 'towny' of his – she came from the same home town – and he just wanted to make sure that she and the children got home safely.

Eventually, after much begging and cajoling from Hughes, Maria Clements agreed to go home at about half-past nine that evening. Hughes accompanied her and the children to her house but, when they got there, Maria was unable to open the door. She went to a neighbour, Mr Davis, to ask for his assistance but when Davis reached the house he found that Hughes had already got the door open. Maria, Hughes and the two children went inside, shutting the door behind them.

Having taken Mr Wyatt's statement, the police went straight to the barracks, where they asked to speak to the three soldiers from the 26th Cameronians Regiment of Foot. When they discovered that Hughes had been absent from his barracks overnight on 4/5 June and had not retuned until twenty minutes to seven on the morning of 5 June, Detective Sergeant William Poole charged him with the wilful murder of a woman in Montague Street. 'I am not the man. I was never in the street,' Hughes protested but he was nevertheless detained on suspicion of having killed Maria Clements. Once at the police station, he was searched and a pair of woman's stockings was removed from his trouser pockets.

Hughes claimed that the stockings had come from a prostitute named either 'Lou' or 'Louey', with whom he had slept on the night of the murder. He told the police that he had been drunk at the time and was therefore unable to remember Lou's address, although he was certain that she lived on Prospect Street. However, when Charles Clements was shown the stockings, he was positive that they belonged to his wife.

An inquest was opened into Maria's death at the Police Court by borough coroner, Mr W.H. Garrington. Having heard all the evidence, the coroner's jury retired but were unable to agree on a verdict. Garrington therefore took the unusual step of adjourning the inquest for a week to allow the members of the jury more time to consider the case. The inquest was resumed on 13 June, with Garrington immediately sending the jury out to continue their deliberations. After debating for more than two hours, the inquest jury informed the coroner that they had concluded that Maria Clements met with her death from violence and that the violence was inflicted by the hands of John Hughes. Garrington then committed Hughes to stand trial for the wilful murder of Maria Clements at the next assizes. By the time the inquest concluded, Hughes had already appeared before magistrates, who had drawn the same conclusions.

The trial opened on 15 July before Mr Justice Keating, with Mr Poulden and Mr Gunner prosecuting and Mr Charles appearing for the defence. Twenty-one-year-old John Hughes had consistently maintained that he had been concerned for the safety of Maria Clements and her children, given that Maria had consumed a considerable quantity of beer in the Queen's Head on the afternoon before her death. He insisted that he had escorted Maria home and that he had put the two children to bed before leaving her to sober up. He had then spent the night with a woman in Prospect Street, returning to his barracks at twenty to seven the next morning. From the very outset of the trial, there was considerable evidence to support Hughes's version of events.

One of the key pieces of evidence against him was the stockings, identified by Charles Clements as having belonged to his wife. By the time the case came to court, Clements had decided that the stockings had not been Maria's after all. Maria had very small feet and was in the habit of cutting the toe end off her stocking and resewing them, but the pair found in Hughes's pockets had been machine stitched rather than hand sewn and did not appear to have been altered in any way.

The only person who might have been able to identify Hughes as the murderer was Maria's oldest daughter. The little girl was brought into court and questioned but denied ever having seen Hughes before. It was obviously a big ordeal for so young a child and Mr Justice Keating was not prepared to allow her to be questioned for too long. He eventually determined that she was far too young to be a reliable witness and directed that the jury should discount her evidence.

The defence called a young prostitute from Prospect Street who told the court that Hughes had arrived at her house around midnight on 4 June and spent the entire night with her, leaving at six o'clock the next morning. The woman stated that a pair of stockings had been taken from her that night and positively identified those found in Hughes's pockets as being hers. Two of Hughes's barrack mates also gave evidence, both stating that they had seen Hughes in Prospect Street at about eleven o'clock on the night of 4 June.

In his closing speech for the defence, Mr Charles pointed out to the jury that Hughes was a young man of good character, with no previous offences to his name. He questioned what possible motive Hughes could have had to murder Maria Clements – nothing had been stolen from her house and, although she had undoubtedly been brutally treated, there was nothing to suggest that she had actually been raped.

In his summary of the evidence for the jury, Mr Justice Keating stated that they should first decide whether or not they believed that Maria Clements had been murdered. He reminded them that, although Maria's young daughter had stated that she had never seen Hughes before, there were numerous witnesses who had seen Hughes with Maria and the children prior to the murder, including pub landlord Mr Wyatt, Privates Parker and O'Neil and neighbour Mr Davis. There was absolutely no doubt that John Hughes was in the pub with Maria Clements on the afternoon before her death, at which time he had been determined to go home with her. The jury must therefore decide whether that meeting between the victim and the defendant had been the prelude to her violent death at his hands.

The jury needed only a short deliberation to return a verdict of 'Guilty of wilful murder' against John Hughes, who was sentenced to death by Mr Justice Keating.

His execution was scheduled for 4 August 1865 but the sentence caused an immediate outcry throughout much of Hampshire. At the same assizes, another murderer, George Broomfield had also been sentenced to death (see chapter 10), although Broomfield was later reprieved on the grounds of insanity. However, in the minds of many Hampshire residents, as an older and obviously more intelligent man, Broomfield was by far the worse of the two killers. While nobody entertained too many sympathetic feelings towards John Hughes, many people felt it unfair that he should be left for execution while Broomfield was reprieved. This sense of 'unfairness' was especially keenly felt by the number of serving soldiers stationed in the area. There were rumours that men from barracks in both Winchester and Portsmouth were planning a mass demonstration in protest, with the aim of disrupting or even preventing the execution.

With this in mind, the prison authorities decided to hold the execution at seven o'clock in the morning rather than at the customary hour of eight o'clock. For obvious reasons, the change of time was not publicised, although all military leave was suspended in the area from 3 August until well after Hughes had been executed.

Thus, Hughes's execution was watched by a relatively small number of people, most of whom were young boys or women with children. Even so, as Hughes walked to the gallows in his distinctive red uniform coat, the crowd were vociferous in making their displeasure known, shouting, 'Where is the other?' and 'Bring out Broomfield.'

Executioner William Calcraft seemed particularly nervous and took an unusually long time in preparing Hughes for execution. When the trap door finally fell, it was evident that Calcraft had miscalculated the length of the rope, since Hughes's head, clad in its black hood, remained level with the floor of the drop. The crowd watched in horror as Hughes struggled convulsively for several minutes while the prison chaplain continued to read the burial service until he was finally still.

Note: Some contemporary sources name Hughes's regiment as the 25th Cameronians rather than the 26th. Research indicates that the regiment was named 26th in 1786, hence I have used that name. The barracks in which the regiment was stationed is named as both Clarence Barracks and Cambridge Barracks. Although the majority of the contemporary newspapers name Charles Clements's ship as HMS *Diadem*, the very first accounts record it as HMS *Asia*. I have assumed that the former name is correct simply because it is mentioned most frequently.

12

'I KNOW WHAT I HAVE DONE AND I AM NOT SORRY FOR IT'

Aldershot, 1869

The 7th Fusiliers had recently been transferred from Liverpool to Aldershot, something that had greatly annoyed Private William Dixon, since he suddenly found himself billeted in a hut with his arch-enemy, Corporal William Brett. Over the years the two men had clashed numerous times after Brett had reported Dixon for trifling breaches of discipline. In fact, Dixon was frequently reported for breaches of discipline by other officers, just as often as by Brett, but for some reason, Brett just seemed to antagonise Dixon. When the two had been placed in the same hut at Liverpool, Dixon had begged his commanding officers to let him change rooms before something dreadful happened and his request had been granted.

Now twenty-eight-year-old Dixon was once more sharing accommodation with Brett in No. 1 Hut, A Lines, South Camp and, on 20 July 1869, just eleven days after Brett and Dixon were first messed together, the 'something dreadful' that Dixon had prophesised actually happened.

Dixon's regiment were in their hut engaged in filling mattresses with clean straw when Dixon and a comrade, Private Henshall, decided that they had had enough, left their duty and sloped off to the canteen for a drink. Corporal James Cross soon noticed their absence and went to the canteen to fetch them back. They returned reluctantly and, as soon as they had finished their duty, went back to the canteen where they both had more drinks.

On getting back to their hut, Henshall picked up his rifle from the rack and, when asked what he was playing at, made several threats against Corporal Brett, saying that he would 'put his lights out before dark'. Dixon took the rifle from Henshall, who was obviously drunk, and replaced it on the rack. Corporal Cross told Henshall that he would have to be reported for picking up his rifle but Dixon insisted that Henshall was too drunk to know what he was doing and asked Cross to turn a blind eye. Cross asked to look at the rifle that Dixon had just replaced and assured himself that it was unloaded. He then went to get someone to escort Henshall to the guardroom, where he could sober up.

Although Dixon had been drinking, he was less noticeably drunk. His bed was at the very end of the hut, behind the door and he was thus partly obscured from the view of his roommates. However, when they heard a click, they turned to see Dixon with his

Snider rifle by his side in the ready position, which was always assumed before the rifle was raised to the shoulder and fired.

Private Benjamin Adams was horrified. 'For God's sake, don't do that,' he told Dixon, asking him to hand over his gun. Dixon refused and Adams bravely tried to take the rifle from him, but Dixon wasn't about to surrender it. 'If you prevent me from doing what I am about to do you shall have the contents instead of him,' he warned Adams, who wisely stepped back two or three paces.

As he did, Adams happened to glance out of the window of the hut and saw Brett walking towards the hut with Corporal Cross. 'For God's sake, don't come in,' Adams shouted, but sadly Brett didn't seem to hear him. As Brett and Cross reached the open door, Adams tried again, yelling at them to 'Go back'. Although Cross clearly heard this warning, Brett either didn't hear or took no notice and, as he walked into the hut, Dixon shouldered his rifle, aimed at the corporal and pulled the trigger. There was a deafening bang and Brett immediately dropped to the floor.

Once again, Adams tried to seize the gun and this time Dixon relinquished it without a fight, telling Adams, 'Let me go. I know what I have done and I am not sorry for it.' Dixon went quietly with Adams and Private Robert Bunce to the guardroom, while others in the hut called for a doctor and tried to administer first aid to Brett.

Sadly, the corporal was beyond any help, having died instantly as a result of a single bullet passing clean through his head.

The civilian police were summoned and Dixon was taken to Winchester Prison. At an inquest held before W.H. Hayley, the Deputy Coroner for North Hampshire, the jury returned a verdict of wilful murder against him and he was committed for trial at the next assizes at Winchester.

High Street, Aldershot. (Author's collection)

In the event, his case was moved from Hampshire to the Old Bailey in order that he should be tried more quickly, and his trial opened before Mr Justice Montague Smith on 18 August. The Attorney General, Sir R.P. Collier prosecuted, assisted by Mr Poland, while Mr Straight defended Dixon, who pleaded 'Not Guilty' to the charge.

Corporal Cross was the first to take the witness stand and, after relating the events of 20 July to the court, he was asked about the characters of the accused and the deceased. Cross described Brett as an exemplary officer and Dixon as a popular, good-natured man, who was inclined to drink.

After hearing evidence from Adams, Bunce and the final resident of No. 1 Hut, John Carter, the next witness to testify was Captain Fitzmaurice Beauchamp, the company commander. Beauchamp listed the number of times that Brett had reported Dixon, the last time being ten days before the murder for being out of his quarters at eleven o'clock at night. Between January and June 1839, Brett had made several similar reports when Dixon had been absent either from parade or from tattoo.

Next to testify was John Gregg, the Deputy Governor of Winchester Gaol who had spoken with Dixon. Dixon had admitted to shooting Brett, who he described as a bully.

George Marsh, the schoolmaster at Winchester Gaol, told the court that, since Dixon could neither read nor write, he had asked Marsh to write to his mother for him. Dixon dictated that Brett was a bully and a tyrant and that drink had been the cause of the murder, for which he expressed regret. Mr Longhirst, an army surgeon, followed Marsh into the witness box and testified to the nature of Brett's injuries.

Mr Straight then addressed the jury for the defence. He conceded that the case was practically a foregone conclusion, since Dixon had confessed to the killing, but asked the jury to consider the question of insanity. Reading from a well-known book on mental health, he quoted several passages to the jury on the subject of homicidal mania and monomania, suggesting that Dixon seemed to exhibit the textbook symptoms of homicidal mania, a murder committed without any forewarning.

Straight reminded the jury that it was Dixon who had disarmed Private Henshall shortly before the shooting had taken place, asking them why he would do that if he had harboured any violent intentions towards Corporal Brett. His calmness – both before and after the shooting – were again indicative of homicidal mania and Dixon had shown no outward animosity towards Brett at the time of the killing and there had been no obvious quarrel between the two men that might have provoked Dixon into shooting. Indeed, his motive for killing Corporal Brett seemed woefully inadequate, if Dixon were completely sane.

The Attorney General then addressed the jury in reply. He first congratulated the counsel for the defence on his handling of the case, while at the same time intimating that Straight was fighting a case so strong that it was almost impossible for him to win. Collier maintained that any suggestion of Dixon's insanity existed only in Straight's imagination, since no medical men had been called upon to examine the accused. Dixon could not even offer drunkenness as an excuse for his actions but was in full possession of his senses when he had taken it into his head to shoot Corporal Brett.

Brett had been universally recognised as a humane, kind-hearted man who was charged by the army with maintaining discipline among the ranks. The ultimate effect of reporting Private Dixon would be that Dixon would be prohibited from going to the canteen while being punished for his breaches of discipline, which, for a man with his undisputed fondness for alcohol, would be a harsh punishment indeed, one that would be likely to stir up deep feelings of revenge.

On the day of the shooting, Henshall had been too drunk to be discreet and keep quiet about his intentions, but Dixon had been sober enough and sane enough to keep his counsel and to surreptitiously load his rifle with the sole purpose of killing Corporal Brett. The Attorney General scoffed at Mr Straight's books, telling the jury that some of the doctors who wrote books would invent a new name for murder if they possibly could. However, in his book, murder was murder and must be punished by the law if human life was to be protected.

Mr Justice Montague Smith then addressed the jury, telling them that they only needed to decide if Dixon had fired his rifle at Corporal Brett feloniously. Addressing the question of insanity, he told the jury that, in the eyes of the law, a man was presumed sane unless the contrary was proved and there had been no attempt by the defence to have Dixon examined by doctors before his trial.

It took the jury just five minutes deliberation to return a verdict of 'Guilty', but with a recommendation for mercy. Promising to pass the recommendation to the appropriate authorities, Mr Justice Montague Smith pronounced the death sentence on William Dixon for the wilful murder of thirty-year-old Corporal William Brett. He added that, in his opinion, the murder had been an especially cruel and cowardly one, since Brett had been given no opportunity to defend himself. Dixon was then returned to Winchester Gaol to await his fate.

On the day before his scheduled execution, Dixon dictated yet another letter to the schoolmaster, which he requested should be made public. Under his instruction, the schoolmaster wrote:

> I, William Dixon, now lying under sentence of death for the wilful murder of Corporal Brett beg to state that my sentence is a just one for the terrible deed I committed and for which I am very sorry. It is my earnest wish to seek forgiveness from the friends of Corporal Brett for the injury I have so unwarrantably inflicted on him, as well as on them by my most wicked act. It is too late now for me to expect any answer to this request, but I hope they may tell my God they have forgiven me; also that my neglect of God and wretched love of drink as well as my evil passions should have led me to such a deed. Surely if soldiers and especially young soldiers could know what misery and wretchedness follow such conduct as mine they would never allow their passions to be their master and continue such a course of drink and other vices as have been my ruin and the cause of my taking a fellow creature's life and a comrade's who deserved a better fate and whose brother was my friend and companion. I now feel I can make no adequate satisfaction for my sin and crime. I fear it is almost useless to hope my fate will provide a warning to many of my comrades and companions in the regiment I belong to. I only wish they knew what I had gone through since I committed the crime. Perhaps then they would not be so likely to imitate my example in this or any other respect. My present anxiety and sorrow have many causes. I have sinned against God all my life. I have wickedly and unjustifiably deprived a fellow creature of life and involved his friends as well as my own in grief and misery. I feel I hardly dare expect forgiveness from man or mercy from God, but for his great love in Christ Jesus and my hope is solely in that Saviour. Had I learned to know more of Him years ago, I might have escaped this shameful end and had a more satisfactory hope in a dying hour. I hope God may have mercy on me for Christ's

sake and I wish that my death may prove a terror and a warning to people and especially to soldiers who are going on as I used to do. [*sic*]

The letter, signed W.M. Dixon, finished with a request that it be shown both to Corporal Brett's brother and to the other men in Dixon's regiment.

This was to be Dixon's last communication, since William Calcraft executed him on 6 September 1869 at Winchester Prison. He was buried within the prison grounds.

To an extent, his dying wishes came true, since immediately after his death, the army reviewed its previous policy of allowing the men to keep ammunition for their rifles in their pouches. It was subsequently ordered that all ammunition should henceforth be stored in a central magazine, a key to which would be given to some responsible person in camp or barracks so that ammunition could be issued in the event of an emergency. Otherwise, ammunition would be distributed to the soldiers only when required for their duties and collected again afterwards. Hopefully, as a result of this review, fewer serving man would be able to succumb to a sudden impulse, as Dixon himself had done.

13

'I DID IT BECAUSE HE SHOULD NOT HAVE HER'

Newtown, Aldershot, 1888

In an upstairs bedroom at the Prince Albert Inn in Newtown, near Aldershot, four children slept peacefully in their beds. The three girls shared one bed, while their eleven-year-old brother slept in a second.

At just after six o'clock on the morning of 6 February 1888, something disturbed young James. He woke suddenly to hear a strange gurgling noise coming from his sisters' bed that sounded as though one of them was struggling desperately for breath. As he sat up in bed he saw, by the light of a lamp burning in the bedroom, eighteen-year-old Annie roll out of bed onto the floor, blood gushing from a wound in her throat. The bedroom door was open and through it James could see his father standing just outside on the landing, an open razor in his hand.

James froze in sheer terror, so afraid of his father that he was unable to move or cry out for help. After what seemed like an eternity to the petrified boy, he heard his mother running upstairs. His father tried to prevent her from going into the bedroom but she pushed past him, falling to her knees next to Annie crying 'Oh! He has murdered my daughter!' At that, his father ran away, grabbing a bottle of brandy from the bar as he left. Annie had died almost instantly from loss of blood, her throat cut so deeply that her head was almost severed from her body.

The police were called and quickly set off in pursuit of forty-two-year-old George Clarke. When the man's neighbours heard what had happened, they too joined in the hunt for the fugitive. Clarke was soon spotted on the banks of the canal about a mile from the inn, his large, extremely ferocious dog at his side. When he realised that he had been seen, he ran for his life, crashing through woods and stumbling through bogs in a desperate effort to escape.

One neighbour, Edward Heddington, who kept the Heroes of Lucknow Inn in North Lane, Aldershot, had saddled up his pony before joining the chase. Being on horseback rather than on foot, he managed to overtake Clarke and laid in wait for him at Ash Church, detaining him until the police caught up. Police Constable Gough then arrested George Clarke, who was surprisingly cooperative. He showed Gough where he had hidden the bloodstained razor in a clump of long grass and, when charged with the murder, he freely admitted it. 'She has drove me to this,' he told Gough, explaining that Annie had recently begun courting a soldier in the Medical Staff Corps. 'I did it because he should not have her.'

Clarke had been married to his wife for about fifteen years and the victim, Annie Vaughan, was his stepdaughter. Annie, who had been three when Clarke had married her mother, had always thought of him as her real father. Clarke had served for twenty-one years in the 1st Leicestershire Regiment in the army before being discharged in June 1886. After his discharge, he had worked as a tailor in Portsmouth before becoming the landlord of the pub.

Throughout his army career, Clarke had been a peaceable man who had won a medal for good conduct. However, since taking on the pub, his character had changed. The business was not going well and Clarke and his wife were becoming increasingly unhappy together. Clarke found solace in drink and this fuelled numerous quarrels and fights with his wife. On more than one occasion, Mrs Clarke had taken the children and left, seeking refuge from her husband's drunken rages, but she had always returned.

When interviewed at the police station, Clarke dropped a bombshell, admitting that, for the past two years, Annie Vaughan had been 'as his wife'. Whether or not Annie willingly entered into this arrangement of improper intimacy was not clear but shortly before her death, she had attracted the attentions of a young soldier, Charles Clark.

Charles had begun walking out with Annie Vaughan in January 1888, much to the distress of her stepfather, who said that he wouldn't allow his daughter to walk out with a private soldier. Charles had persisted in trying to court Annie and, on the Sunday before her murder, had succeeded in obtaining grudging permission from Clarke to go out for a walk with her.

Clarke seemed to be very gradually coming round to the idea that Annie had a beau but seemed most concerned that, should he object to the relationship too strongly, Charles would marry Annie and take her away. Charles told Clarke that he had no intention of marrying while he was still a private, adding that, if Clarke would keep off the drink then there would be fewer arguments between them. However, the apparent truce between the two men didn't last for long and, when Charles and Annie returned from their walk it was to find an angry Clarke waiting for them. There was yet another row, which culminated in Clarke ordering Charles to stay away from his house and his daughter.

On the night before the murder, Clarke had gone into the bedroom shared by his four children and kissed them all goodnight. He had then spent much of the night pacing about downstairs in the pub, before slipping quietly into the bedroom early the next morning and silently cutting Annie's throat.

Clarke was brought for trial at the Winchester Assizes before Mr Justice Field, charged with 'feloniously, wilfully and of malice aforethought killing and murdering Annie Vaughan at Aldershot on the 6 February'. As would have been expected, he pleaded 'Not Guilty' to the charge against him but, in view of his previous confession to the murder, his trial was a mere formality.

Mr Temple Cooke, for the prosecution, outlined the facts of the case before calling in turn James and thirteen-year-old Lily Clarke, the half brother and sister of the dead girl. Both described the events of the early morning of 6 February, their accounts matching almost word for word. Lily testified to the frequent quarrels in the family, the most recent being in the week of the murder, when her father had told her mother and Annie that he was going to bring another woman home. According to Lily, Annie had been the most angered by this and had told her father that she would not stay in the house if he did. She and her mother had walked out after the argument on 1 February but both had returned four days later, on the day before Annie's death.

Edward Heddington and Constable Gough were the next witnesses to be called, both recounting the frantic pursuit and eventual arrest of George Clarke. Finally, Charles Clark told of his burgeoning relationship with Annie Vaughan, and Dr Schoolbred from Aldershot testified to the extent of her injuries.

It was then left to the defence counsel, Mr Willes, to address the jury, having called no witnesses for the defence. After telling the jury of Clarke's military service and his previous good character, Willes reminded them that 'misfortunes' seemed to have overtaken the prisoner in his business about the time of the murder. It was all too easy to imagine a man caught in a downward course indulging in drink and, in the delirium of intoxication, being led to committing crimes that he would not think of for a moment when sober. Yet, in this case, there was no evidence of intoxication. Even though Clarke was known to drink to excess and to become argumentative under the influence of alcohol, both Heddington and PC Gough had testified that, when apprehended, Clarke appeared perfectly sober.

If, said Willes, there was no evidence of intoxication then the jury must question whether a man could possibly be sane and commit such a deed. Willes maintained that the evidence indicated that Clarke had been suffering from a 'temporary derangement' at the time of the killing of his stepdaughter.

In his summary of the case, Mr Justice Field described it as 'the clearest case of murder that had ever come before him,' saying that the defence had not raised any issues that would lead to a reduction of the charge against Clarke to one of manslaughter. It was Clarke's duty to protect his wife's daughter, but instead of protecting Annie Vaughan, Clarke had cruelly taken her life.

The Great Hall, Winchester – site of the assizes. (Author's collection)

The jury almost immediately returned a verdict of 'Guilty' and Mr Justice Field addressed the prisoner, saying that in twelve years he had never tried a sadder or more shocking case and all that remained for him to do was to pass sentence of death.

Clarke took the news calmly and was still calm when he was executed by James Berry at Winchester on 27 March 1888. Throughout his trial, the prosecution had insisted that jealousy of Charles Clark was the motive behind the murder of Annie – if George Clarke couldn't have her, then nobody could. It is also apparent that, with Annie Vaughan starting what seemed to be a serious relationship with another man, the details of her illicit relationship with her stepfather were in danger of becoming public. Was George Clarke a jealous man, a man deeply in love, or simply a frightened man? Was Annie a willing participant in the 'improper intimacy' between them or a victim of sexual abuse, for whom Charles Clark represented her first chance to escape from an obsessive and unhealthy relationship? And what part did Mrs Clarke play in the events leading up to the murder? Was she completely ignorant of the relationship between her husband and her daughter or did she simply turn a blind eye to their intimacy?

Sadly the answers to these questions will never be known and all that can be reliably established by reading the newspapers of the time is that an eighteen-year-old girl was cruelly murdered while she slept, by the one man who she should have been able to count on to protect her and keep her safe.

14

'I AM WATCHED ALL OVER THE PLACE LIKE A CLOCK WATCH'

Portsmouth, 1888

On Sunday, 26 August 1888, a steady stream of customers called at a house in St Mary's Road, Portsmouth, expecting to be shaved by barber and hairdresser Thomas Jones. Yet their knocks on the door went unanswered and, although Thomas was normally up and about by seven o'clock in the morning, by half-past two in the afternoon there had been no signs that he was at home.

Mrs Mary Rogers, who lived next door to Thomas Jones, remarked to a visitor that she was becoming concerned about her neighbour. The visitor, Fanny Cook, offered to go and see if anything was wrong and walked through the shared backyard to the rear of Mrs Rogers' and Mr Jones' house. Jones' back door was locked and, although Fanny called out several times, nobody came to the door. Eventually, Fanny peered in through the kitchen window. She could see nothing, apart from a solitary hand resting limply on the fender.

The police were alerted and Inspector William Porter and Sergeant Fry were sent to investigate the unusual occurrences at St Mary's Road. They found all the doors of the house securely locked but Porter spotted that one of the bedroom windows was ajar and, borrowing a set of stepladders, he managed to climb through it.

The house was deathly quiet and the bed, which was made up for just one person, obviously hadn't been slept in. Porter made his way cautiously downstairs and, as he entered the kitchen, he recoiled in horror at the gruesome sight that met his eyes. The entire floor was awash with blood – as the local paper was later to describe it, '... covered with a carpet of slippery gore.' In the midst of the carnage lay the bodies of a man and a woman, their throats cut. The man was Thomas Jones, the woman his estranged wife, Eliza.

The couple had married on 9 April 1886 and, by all accounts, had lived happily together until just six weeks earlier. Eliza was a former prostitute with a fondness for drink and she had apparently been having an affair with a soldier from the Royal Artillery, named Mr Rawlinson.

Eliza Jones made little attempt to be discreet in her dalliance with Gunner Rawlinson and, indeed, almost flaunted their relationship, often staying out all night, or drinking

View of Portsmouth. (Author's collection)

The Town Hall from Victoria Park, Portsmouth, 1920. (Author's collection)

with her lover in the Naval and Military Arms, a pub situated almost opposite the house she shared with her husband. It was inevitable that Thomas Jones would find out about his wife's affair and, six weeks earlier, he had walked into the pub and found Eliza and Rawlinson there together.

'I have found you out now,' he shouted triumphantly, before throwing punches at Eliza and Rawlinson, knocking both of them to the floor. Eliza immediately left him but, almost a month later, Thomas met her again by chance, walking down Lake Road with a soldier.

Thomas began to remonstrate with Eliza about her disgraceful conduct and, once again, raised his hands to her. This time, Eliza went to the magistrates, accusing Thomas of assault and, on 14 August, he was summoned to court and bound over for the sum of £10, to keep the peace towards her.

The fact that Eliza had left Thomas seemed to upset him far less than her all too frequent presence in his local pub, in the company of other men. Eliza seemed to be deliberately taunting her husband with her infidelity and Thomas was hurting. 'You can love and you can hate,' he told a neighbour in the week before his death. 'I hope she will never come nigh me again. I hope she will stay away and then I shall be quite happy. As much as I love her.'

On one occasion, Thomas tried to visit Eliza at her lodgings to plead with her to come back to him and 'live quietly'. Eliza wasn't at home at the time of her husband's visit but Thomas spoke to her landlady, Ellen Rogers, telling her 'I'll be the death of her.' Just two weeks before his death, Thomas tried to sell all his furniture, with the intention of moving away from the area. 'If I stop here, she'll drive me to kill her and myself too', he told prospective purchaser Mr Newbury. Jones was known throughout the area as a quiet, steady and sober man but Newbury was later to say that his manner seemed 'strange', his eyes were rolling and he didn't seem to be in a normal state of mind.

On the evening of 25 August, Eliza Jones was drinking in the Naval and Military Arms with a friend, Kate Whelan. The drink flowed freely and, during the course of the evening, the landlord, Charles Ashby Adams, heard Eliza making nasty remarks about her husband, calling him horrible names and saying that she would never go back to him. However, when the pub closed at 10.30 p.m., she announced her intention of calling at her former home to pick up some of her clothes.

When Eliza first left Thomas, widow Susan Miller, who lodged next door with Mary Rogers, offered to help him with his housework and shopping. At 10.30 p.m. on the night of 25 August, Thomas gave her a penny and asked her to buy him some cheese. Fifteen minutes later, he called in at the pub and purchased a quart of ale, which he took away in a jug. Witnesses from the pub were later to say that he was completely sober at the time but that he appeared pale and agitated, to the point where he was actually trembling.

Susan Miller bought the cheese straight away and returned to deliver it to Thomas. However, as she approached his house, she noticed that the front door was ajar and she could hear the sounds of an argument coming from within. She heard a woman's voice, which she recognised as Eliza's, saying, 'I am watched all over the place like a clock watch.'

Mrs Miller decided not to interfere and took the cheese home with her. 'Eliza's come back. There is high words and I won't go in' she told Mrs Rogers somewhat unnecessarily, since Mrs Rogers could hear the noisy dispute next door for herself, through the walls of her house. The argument continued for some time but, since such quarrels between Thomas and Eliza were nothing out of the ordinary, Mrs Rogers took little notice. Eliza had called at her husband's home several times in the weeks since their separation and Mary Rogers had heard her subjecting him to torrents of vicious verbal abuse, although Thomas usually listened calmly and quietly, without retaliating.

By 11.45 p.m. the street was silent again and Mrs Rogers went to bed. She was a heavy sleeper and heard nothing more from next door. Indeed, nobody heard any further sounds emanating from Thomas Jones' home, the reason for which became evident when the bodies were discovered the next day.

An inquest was opened into the deaths of Thomas and Eliza Jones by Mr T.A. Bramsdon, the Portsmouth coroner. The jury was required to view the bodies in situ, something that caused a slight problem since the house was so small that, in order to see both bodies, the jury would need to have stepped over one of them. In the end, Mary Rogers allowed them to walk through her house to the rear of the premises and Eliza's body was viewed from the back of the house, while Thomas was inspected from the front.

Both Thomas and Eliza were fully dressed, although Eliza had removed her hat, which sat on a low table by the window and Thomas had taken off his jacket, collar and tie, which hung on the back of a chair. The house was poorly furnished and showed no evidence that any struggle had taken place there. The two bodies both had large, gaping wounds in their throats and there was a single bloody handprint on the wall where Eliza had obviously briefly leaned for support before falling to the floor.

The bodies were formally identified by Mrs Mary Whittaker, the sister of thirty-nine-year-old Thomas. Mrs Whittaker told the inquest that their older brother had been 'out of his mind' for the past eight years but that Thomas had always seemed quiet and rational. However, both he and twenty-nine-year-old Eliza were of 'a passionate disposition' and, in combination with Eliza's drinking, this caused some fiery arguments between them, especially since Eliza had walked away from her marriage six weeks earlier.

The inquest heard from several of the residents of St Mary's Road, including the landlord and staff of the Naval and Military Arms, then the two investigating police officers. The last witness to testify was surgeon Mr Frederick Morley, who had seen the bodies on the Sunday afternoon.

Morley stated that Eliza's throat had been cut from ear to ear and that the wound was so deep that her vertebrae had been nicked. A chain that she wore around her neck had been deeply embedded in the wound but, apart from a slight scratch on one of her thumbs, there were no other marks of violence found on the rest of her body. Thomas had a four-inch long wound across the front of his throat and had died from a combination of blood loss and suffocation, caused by the blood from his throat entering his lungs.

An open razor found at the scene had several notches on its blade, which Morley theorised had been made by it coming into contact with Eliza's vertebrae. There was no blood on Eliza's hands, leading Morley to conclude that her wound could not have been self-inflicted. Thomas's hands however were drenched in blood and the surgeon was therefore of the opinion that he had cut both his own and Eliza's throats. The oil lamp and the candle in the room had both been extinguished, so Thomas must have cut his own throat in the dark.

Not unexpectedly, the coroner's jury returned a verdict of murder and suicide by Thomas Jones while in an unsound state of mind. At the conclusion of the inquest, all that remained to be done was to bury Thomas and Eliza and their funerals took place on the Wednesday after their deaths.

Sympathetic neighbours clubbed together to pay for Thomas's funeral, while Eliza's was paid for by Mrs Hawkins, the widow of a previous landlord of the Naval and Military Arms. Separated in life and now also in death, Eliza and Thomas Jones were interred in different cemeteries, she in the Portsea Cemetery at Kingston and he in the Highland Road Cemetery at Easton.

It was widely believed that Thomas Jones was a good, respectable man who had been driven almost to madness by his wife's shameful behaviour. However, while Eliza's funeral passed without incident, Revd G. Edwards refused to perform the full burial service in the mortuary chapel at Thomas's funeral and thus Thomas was sent to his final resting place with just one collect, a Benediction and a repetition of the Lord's Prayer.

The neighbours, who had paid for a full service, were incensed. They pleaded with Edwards to reconsider, pointing out that he had been well paid for his work but Edwards was adamant. What Thomas Jones had done put him 'outside the pale of the Church' and, as a Christian minister, he did not feel justified in reading the whole of the burial service over his remains, especially those parts relating to eternal life, since he did not believe that Jones would go to heaven.

Mr Miller, the neighbour who had actually organised the funeral, took it upon himself to act as spokesperson for all those who had contributed financially. He argued furiously, telling Edwards that a jury of his peers had agreed that Thomas Jones was insane at the time of the murder and, as an insane man, he was not held accountable in law for his actions. Edwards' high-handed attitude was seen as an affront to those neighbours who had clubbed together to pay for a respectable funeral and now unanimously believed that they were not getting what they had paid for. An angry altercation followed and, with extreme difficulty, Mr Miller eventually persuaded his fellow mourners to leave the graveside. By that time, several of them were threatening Edwards with violence but Miller contented himself with a final appeal to the vicar's conscience and a promise that he would be hearing more of the matter.

15

'THERE'S A MAN KILLING A BOY ROUND YONDER!'

Havant, 1888

Between six o'clock and half-past six on the evening of 26 November 1888, eleven-year-old Robert Husband met eight-year-old Percy Knight Searle returning from Randall's shop on the corner of North Street and The Pallant in Havant after running an errand for his mother. Minutes later, terrible screams were heard coming from the direction which Percy would have taken on his journey home.

Robert ran up to the first adult he saw, Mr Henry Shirley, an assistant in Randall's who was standing in the shop doorway. 'There's a man killing a boy round yonder!' he told him before rushing up to carpenter Mr John Platt, who lived nearby and telling him the same thing. Platt immediately went to check Robert's story. Taking Platt's hand, Robert led him a short way up the road before pointing into the darkness and saying, 'There he is.' Telling Husband to go for the police, Platt rushed forward for a closer look, finding a young boy slumped against some railings barely alive, with blood gushing from his nose and mouth. Even as Platt bent to tend to Percy Searle, the boy gasped twice and then died from a combination of shock and loss of blood from wounds to his throat.

Meanwhile, Robert Husband had gone home. Fortunately, Platt knew where he lived and, at the request of the police, agreed to go and fetch him. Platt was unable to get any response when he knocked at the front door of Robert's home, so he went round to the back door and tried again. This time, Robert's father answered the door.

'Where is your boy?' Platt asked.

Mr Husband called for his son, who appeared from inside the house with wet hands.

'You must come with me,' Platt told him and, as soon as he had dried his hands, Robert willingly accompanied him back to the scene of the murder. Asked by the police if he had seen anything, Robert told them that he had seen a tall man in a black coat running away in the direction of The Fairfield.

The police immediately began a search of the area. Some officers were deployed to check outbuildings and unoccupied properties, while others were sent to the station at Havant, on the supposition that the murderer might try to flee the area as soon as possible.

By nine o'clock that evening, both facets of the investigation seemed to have been successful. A two-bladed pocket knife had been found roughly eight yards from where

Percy died. The smaller blade, which was folded in the closed position, was broken in half, whereas the longer was open and covered in blood from handle to tip. Meanwhile, a man named Thomas Clarke had been arrested at Havant station as he was about to board a train leaving for Portsmouth.

Clarke, who was deaf, told the police that he was an engineer and was currently working at Emsworth Brewery. He had come to Havant with a friend but they had become separated and he believed his companion had caught an earlier train home. Clarke's story was subsequently verified but not until he had been charged and brought before a special sitting of magistrates at Havant on the day after the murder.

Right: *North Street, Havant in the 1960s. (Author's collection)*

Below: *West Street, Havant. (Author's collection)*

Once Clarke had been formally discharged, the police arrested several suspects but all were released having been able to account for their movements at the crucial time. On 28 November, the press announced that the investigating officers were seeking two people in connection with the brutal killing.

The first of these was a man seen by a station porter at about 6.35 p.m. on the night of the murder, scrambling aboard the train from Havant to Brighton, without having first bought a ticket. The porter, Alfred Steele, had not heard about the murder at the time and had therefore taken no particular notice of the man's apparent rush to get away, apart from remarking to a colleague that the man's behaviour was highly unusual.

The second man was a hotel guest from Emsworth, who was known to have left there for Havant on the morning of the murder. The guest's conduct throughout his stay had been decidedly odd, so much so that staff had nicknamed him 'The Ripper', after the infamous 'Jack the Ripper', who was believed to have butchered five prostitutes in the Whitechapel area of London between August and November 1888 and whose fiendish exploits, reported in the popular press, had captured the interest of the whole country. 'The Ripper' was expected to return to the hotel after his trip to Havant but the luggage he had left there remained uncollected. A man matching his description was later seen approaching the hotel but was followed by a crowd of suspicious people and did not go inside. Instead, he headed towards Chichester, managed to shake off his pursuers, and was never seen again.

The information about 'The Ripper' was given particular credence by the police in view of a letter received by the Chief Magistrate at the police courts in Whitechapel. Those involved with the hunt for 'Jack' had already received several taunting letters, purporting to come from the killer and this one read:

No 1, England, 1888.
Dear Boss, – It is no good for you to look for me in London, because I am not there. Don't trouble yourself about me till I return, which will not be very long. I like the job too well to leave it long. Oh, it was such a jolly job the last one. i had plenty of time to do it properly, ha! ha! The next lot I mean to do with Vengeance, cut off their head and arms. You think it is the man with the black moustach. Ha! ha! ha! when I have done another you can catch me. So good-bye, dear Boss, till I return. – Yours, Jack the Ripper [sic].

Emsworth, 1960s.
(Author's collection)

The letter, which was dated a few days before Percy's murder, had a Portsmouth postmark and, if it were genuine, seemed to indicate that 'Jack' might have been in Hampshire at the time of Percy's killing.

Many local people believed that 'Jack the Ripper' was responsible for killing Percy, although a post-mortem examination on the boy, conducted by Dr S. Quinton Bond, found that his throat had been rather clumsily slashed four times by a person who was either standing behind him or kneeling over the body. The direction of all of the cuts ran from right to left, indicating that they had been made by a right-handed person. Initially, an attempt had been made to cut Percy's throat with the blade of the knife but, when this had failed, the perpetrator had plunged the point of the knife into Percy's throat to a depth of three inches and pulled it sharply upwards, severing his carotid artery and causing him to lose several pints of blood. The ineptness of execution hardly seemed consistent with the work of a man who had already killed and mutilated five times, particularly as 'Jack' appeared to target only women. However, before long another rumour was spreading around Havant like wild fire. It was said on the streets that someone had confessed to the murder of Percy Searle and that the person who had confessed was Robert Husband.

An inquest was opened into Percy's death on 28 November at the Havant Workhouse by county coroner Mr Goble. Dr Quinton Bond stated that the four cuts on the dead boy's throat had been somewhat ragged, as if they had been made by a bayonet or a knife, rather than a razor. The inquest then heard from Mr Platt, who related finding Percy bleeding to death.

Robert Husband was waiting to give evidence at the inquest but the coroner surprisingly adjourned the proceedings before he was called and he was allowed to go home, where he was almost immediately arrested by Sergeant Knapton and charged with Percy's murder.

'I never did it,' he insisted.

Taken to the police station, Robert was examined by Superintendent Kinsholt, who noticed blood on the back of his right wrist and on the right-hand cuff of his shirt. Asked to explain its presence, Robert told the Superintendent that he had cut himself. 'This is the cut, Sir,' he stated, showing Kinsholt a small cut on the front of his wrist. Kinsholt noted that the cut had scabbed over and believed it to be several days old.

Robert was asked to surrender his scarf, which he did very reluctantly. More blood-like stains were found on the scarf and later on a handkerchief at his home, although since this was dark red in colour, it was difficult to determine exactly what the stains were.

When questioned, Robert made several conflicting statements to the police, the main one being that he had been standing by a street lamp and had seen the murder being committed by a tall man wearing a dark coat and a high hat, who had then run away. Sergeant Knapton and Detective Lawler immediately went back to the scene of the murder and, while Lawler positioned himself at the exact spot where the body had been found, Knapton went to where Robert said he had been standing and found that he could not see his colleague. Robert changed his story, now saying that he had been to see a Mrs Farnden to collect some money on behalf of his father and had watched the murder from her doorway. Again, the police recreated the scene and once more demonstrated that Robert could not possibly have witnessed the murder. Mrs Farnden also denied having seen him on the night in question.

The police questioned Robert's older brother, George, who told them that the knife found near to Percy's body on the night of the murder belonged to him. He had mislaid the knife, which he normally kept in his jacket pocket, on the day of the murder. The knife had been given to him only the previous week by a friend, Thomas Stevens, and, when Stevens was shown the knife, he too positively identified it as the one that he had given to George.

The police also found several witnesses who stated that they had seen the knife in Robert's possession. Errand boy Henry Wheeler told the police that he recognized the knife as one that Robert had tried to sell him on the morning before the murder. Robert had asked for a penny for the knife but, on inspecting it, Henry had spotted the broken blade and decided that he didn't want it. Robert had then tried to swap knives with labourer John Smith. Albert Farrell had also seen Robert with the knife and the police also found a witness, Charles Clark, who told them that, on the night of the murder, Robert had approached him, brandishing his knife and saying, 'Here comes Jack the Ripper!' A seven-year-old girl named Ethel Whitbread stated that she had seen Robert sharpening a knife on the morning of the murder. Asked by the police what he had done with his knife, Robert initially refused to tell them. He eventually said that he had given it away and, when asked to whom he had given it, changed his statement to say that he had lost it.

With the evidence against him mounting, Robert Husband was brought before a special sitting of the Havant County Bench, charged with the murder of Percy Knight Searle. The hearing was adjourned pending the results of further enquiries and Robert was remanded in custody.

The inquest into Percy's death re-opened on 5 December and was further adjourned until 8 December. When it resumed, one of the first people to speak was solicitor George Feltham, who had been retained for Husband's defence. It was quite outside his experience, said Feltham, for someone to be charged with murder before the inquest had determined how the deceased person actually died.

Captain Boyd of the Submarine Miners Militia, who was also a local magistrate, told the inquest that he had passed the spot where Percy's body was found at 5.50 p.m. on the night of the murder. Had Percy's body been there then, said Boyd, he would definitely have seen it, even though it was pitch dark at the time and pouring with rain. Boyd had not heard Percy's desperate screams, nor had he seen either Percy or Robert. He had, however, met a man, who he described as having the appearance of a 'navvy', heading in the direction of the place where Percy died. Boyd described the man as about 5ft 9in or 5ft 10in tall but stated that he would not be able to recognize him again. Taken back to the crime scene by Detective Inspector Lawler,

Boyd measured the distance between where he had seen the man and the location of Percy's body, finding it to be fifty-three paces.

The inquest next heard from a boy named William Farnden. Farnden had already appeared at the magistrates' court when Robert was first charged but the magistrates had refused to hear his evidence on the grounds that he didn't understand the nature of an oath. Farnden had presumably since been schooled in the correct responses, as he was now able to satisfy the coroner that he understood what was expected of him. He told the inquest that, on the night of the murder, he had left home at about five o'clock to go to Mrs Randall's shop. While he was there, Percy had entered the shop and, moments later, Farnden saw Robert Husband peeping through the door.

William was the first to leave the shop and, when he went outside, Robert Husband was there. William and Robert walked down The Pallant together and spent a minute or so messing around in the yard of the Bear Hotel before separating outside Farnden's home, which was only a short distance from the spot where Percy had met his death.

The final witness at the inquest was Percy's mother, who told the coroner that Percy and Robert had recently had a minor quarrel, after which Robert had threatened to kick her son.

Although the inquest was adjourned again, when it was resumed on 12 December, the coroner's jury returned a verdict of wilful murder by person or persons unknown. However, by then the magistrates had already committed Robert Husband for trial at the next assizes at Winchester.

His trial opened on 19 December 1888, before Mr Justice Stephen. Mr Temple Cooke and Mr Rubie appeared for the prosecution, while Mr Charles Mathews and Mr Bovill Smith defended Robert, who was then just eleven years and eleven months old.

The prosecution first outlined the facts of the case as they saw them. Various witnesses, including William Farnden and Mr Platt, had seen Robert Husband in the vicinity of the scene of the crime at around the time of Percy's murder. Mr Shirley had been serving in Randall's shop and, as he stood in the doorway, he saw Robert running towards him. Robert had shouted that a man was killing a boy and the shout had attracted the attention of Platt who lived almost opposite the shop and had gone to see if he could find the young victim.

The prosecution called a number of witnesses to give evidence on the knife, including George Husband, who testified to owning it briefly and then losing it. Under cross-examination by the defence, George admitted that, shortly before discovering that he had mislaid the knife, he had walked past the exact spot where Percy's body was later found. However, the impact of this revelation on the jury was weakened by the fact that, when found, the knife had been heavily bloodstained.

Witnesses were called to dispute the contradictory statements that Robert Husband had made while in custody, when he insisted that he had seen a tall man committing the murder. The prosecution maintained that the tall man had been invented by Robert in order to deflect suspicion from himself. It was shown that it was impossible for Robert to have seen anything from any of the places where he told the police he had been standing.

The court then heard from Dr Quinton Bond and Home Office analyst Professor Charles M. Tidy, who had been sent the knife and several items of Robert's clothing for testing on 30 November.

Quinton Bond told the court that, in his opinion, a young boy like the defendant would have possessed sufficient strength to inflict the wounds in Percy's throat. Tidy stated that the blood on the knife was 'living blood' but he could not determine whether it originated from a human or an animal. With regard to the blood found on Robert's shirt cuff, Tidy believed it to be at least a month old and he had found no other bloodstains on any of the clothes submitted to him by the police. The towel, which Mr Platt had seen Robert using to dry his hands shortly after the murder, had been washed by Robert's mother before being taken by the police for testing and also bore no evidence of bloodstaining.

Counsel for the defence, Charles Mathews, seized on Professor Tidy's evidence, saying that it was just part of the reason why the jury should acquit his client and give him back his liberty.

Mathews went on to say that, despite some variations in his statements, Robert had consistently stuck to his original story, in which he had said that he had seen a tall man killing Percy Searle and then running away. Mathews then spoke about the timing of events on the evening of 26 November, saying that there had been some question about whether or not Robert had actually entered William Farnden's house. Conflicting evidence on this point had been given by the Farnden family and Mathews bemoaned the fact that Farnden's sister, who was in the house at the time, had not been called as a witness. Regardless of whether Robert had been into William's house or had been left outside, the two boys had obviously spent some time together while Percy was still in the shop and Mathews questioned Robert's ability to get back there in time to accost and murder Percy as he walked home. Robert's father, also named Robert, and his stepmother, Fanny, had already testified that the boy had left home at about five minutes to six and returned at about twenty past, having collected some money from Mrs Farnden and that there had been no blood on his person or clothes on his return.

Mathews pointed out that there was only one inch difference between Robert's height and that of his alleged victim. Furthermore, there were no signs that any struggle had taken place at the scene of the crime. This suggested that a man had committed the murder, since Percy had obviously been approached from behind and taken by surprise. Would Robert have been big and strong enough to kill Percy in this manner, asked Mathews, apparently discounting Dr Quinton Bond's earlier testimony that he would.

Nobody who had seen Robert in the immediate aftermath of Percy's killing had noticed any blood on his hands or clothing and no blood had been found by subsequent testing. John Platt had taken the boy's hand as Robert led him to the murder scene and had stated in court that it was dry at the time. There was no real motive for Robert to commit the crime, other than a childish falling-out with Percy and, with regard to the knife, there was absolutely no proof that the knife seen in Robert's possession prior to the killing was the murder weapon.

Finally, Mathews alluded to the murders committed in London by the unidentified killer known as 'Jack the Ripper'. He reminded the jury of the letter allegedly sent by 'Jack' with a Portsmouth postmark and of the suspicious behaviour of the hotel guest at Emsworth, who had never been back to reclaim his luggage. Several trains left Havant station immediately after the murder and the real killer could easily have been on one of them.

It was then left for Mr Justice Stephen to sum up the evidence for the jury, a process that took almost three hours. He referred first of all to Robert Husband's age, quoting from the book *Digest of the Criminal Law*, which stated: 'No act done by any person over seven and under fourteen is a crime, unless it be shown affirmatively that such person had sufficient capacity to know that the act was wrong.' Should the jury find Robert guilty, they must be completely satisfied that he had some conception of the wickedness of the act and its awful consequences.

Mr Justice Stephen cited a recent case in Exeter, where a twelve-year-old girl had been tried for the murder of a four-year-old. He asked the jury to cast their minds back to when they were eleven years old and to recall the thoughts and feelings they had experienced then.

The judge then dealt with the timing of the events of the night of the murder. Percy Searle had been seen alive at six o'clock in the evening and at twenty-three minutes past six Sergeant Knapton had arrived to begin investigating his murder. Had Robert killed Percy, he would have had to attack Percy within seconds of parting company with William Farnden, otherwise his story of seeing a man committing the murder could well be true. However, the judge then questioned why Robert had not returned to the Farnden's home to raise the alarm, rather than running in the opposite direction, down The Pallant.

Platt had seen Robert immediately after the murder had occurred and had clearly stated that there was no blood on his hands or clothes at the time, neither had any blood subsequently been found on his garments by the Home Office analyst.

Next, Mr Justice Stephen addressed the matter of the knife. There was little doubt that the knife found within yards of Percy's body on the night of the murder was the murder weapon. It was smothered in blood and fitted perfectly into the wounds on Percy's throat. There was satisfactory evidence that the knife had been given to Robert's brother, George and there was even evidence to suggest that Robert had an opportunity to take it from his brother's jacket. However, the jury must be convinced that the murder weapon and the knife given to George Husband were one and the same.

The jury retired for fifteen minutes, before returning to pronounce Robert Husband 'Not Guilty' of the murder of Percy Knight Searle. Robert was discharged and returned home, where he was met by a huge crowd of people wishing to congratulate him on the verdict. Such was the public belief in his innocence that a collection amounting to more than £70 had been organised to pay for his defence.

The murder of Percy Knight Searle remains unsolved to this day, although rumours that it was the work of 'Jack the Ripper' have persisted. In *The Times* of 27 November 1888, there is an intriguing mention of some writing found on a shutter in Hanover Street in Portsmouth, which appears to suggest a connection between 'Jack the Ripper' and the murder of Percy Searle – unfortunately, I have been unable to verify the existence of this writing nor to find out what was written. Of course, the identity of the man who became perhaps the most infamous murderer in British history is also still a complete mystery.

However, two people whose names have been suggested as being the perpetrator of the 'Jack the Ripper' murders in London were known to have connections with Hampshire. The first of these was trained doctor and journalist Robert D'Onston Stephenson, aka Roslyn D'Onston, who moved to the East End of London from Brighton in July 1888. (It must be remembered that the man seen by porter Mr Steele at Havant station on the night of the murder was hurriedly boarding a train to Brighton.) There is evidence to suggest that Stephenson was living in Portsmouth for a period of eight months at around the time of the murder of Percy Searle. Yet, at the same time, there is also conflicting evidence to suggest that he was in fact a private patient at the London Hospital, Whitechapel, staying there from July to December 1888.

Another man suspected of being 'Jack' was James Maybrick, who was himself a murder victim having allegedly been poisoned by his wife, Florence, in 1889. Maybrick had family links with Hampshire and his brother, Michael, lived on the Isle of Wight, serving as the mayor of Ryde between 1900 and 1911.

Given that Jack the Ripper's predilection was for murdering women and that his preferred hunting ground was Whitechapel in London, it seems unlikely that he should target a young boy in Havant, Hampshire, particularly in view of the fact that Percy's throat was said to have been cut 'clumsily'. Thus, the only thing that is certain about the case is that, whoever killed Percy Knight Searle will have long gone to his own grave, taking his dark secret with him.

Note: Percy's name is often alternately spelled Serle in contemporary newspaper accounts of the murder. The name of the man who found his body is alternatively given as John Platt and John Pratt and his occupation described as a carpenter or a dairyman. I have used the most common spelling variations for both. There is also some discrepancy about witness William Farnden who is described both as a boy who spent time with Robert on the night of the murder and who did not understand the nature of an oath and also as a labourer who went to buy coal from Husband's yard on the afternoon of the murder.

16

'I AM THE VICTIM OF A TERRIBLE INFATUATION'

Stamshaw, Portsmouth, 1891

Edward Henry Fawcett Watts married Esther Emily Hickley in 1875. Having served for several years in the Royal Artillery, Watts then joined the navy, becoming an able seaman. However, in 1887, Watts was invalided out of the navy on a pension, which he supplemented by working as a labourer. By 1891, he was working at a gas works in London and he and Esther were living in New Cross with their four-year-old son, Arthur, who was the only surviving child of the seven born during their marriage.

After being discharged from the navy, Edward Watts became addicted to drink. Normally a polite, well-conducted man and a good husband and father, under the influence of alcohol he became excitable and quarrelsome. Esther and Edward rowed continuously about his drinking, particularly since, as his drinking increased, he grew less and less inclined to work and the couple were soon relying on Esther's wage as a laundress to feed and clothe themselves and pay rent. On more than one occasion, the fighting between them became physical and, in June 1890, while the couple were living in Greenwich, Watts was bound over by magistrates to keep the peace after assaulting Esther.

Esther left Edward after this but, as he had done many times before, Watts promised his wife faithfully that he would give up drinking and she agreed to give him another chance. Their marriage limped on until March of 1891, when Esther's sister went to stay with the couple. Overhearing a violent row between them, she burst into their bedroom to find Edward attempting to strangle Esther and threatening to kill her in such a way that no doctor in England would know how she died.

That argument was the last straw for Esther and she packed up what things she could carry and took Arthur back to her father's home in Twyford Avenue, Stamshaw. She found a job at the Brunswick Laundry and set about making a new life for herself and her son.

However, Edward Watts was not one to give up easily and bombarded his wife with letters, promising Esther that he had found work and stopped drinking for good and begging her to give him just one last chance. At first Esther ignored his pleas but she eventually responded.

Edward and Esther Watts, 1891.

THE MURDERER.

THE VICTIM.

Edward replied the very next day:

1st April 1891
I now send these few lines in answer to your letter I received last night and I am sorry to think you will not look over it on the conditions I mentioned, which I think you have misunderstood. I told you if I was in good work and kept myself as a man should do and would during the whole of the time send you as much money as I could every week also my pension every quarter as I get it. Could you look over it then, as this living away from you is killing me by inches and I own, it is all my own fault.

The letter continued to say that Edward intended to visit his wife and son in Portsmouth unless he received a letter from her by return of post telling him not to come. It was signed 'Your loving and broken-hearted husband, E. Watts.'

Edward wrote to Esther again on 3 April, telling her that he was in Portsmouth and asking her to bring his son to see him and saying that he wanted to talk to her on important business. Watts now signed his letter 'Yours etc E. Watts' and the letter ended ominously: 'Send word back by the bearer "Yes" or "No", as I shall go to my lodgings if you don't come and see me or tell me when you will come. I will not be ansrible for my actions' [sic]. Watts then added a PS, bemoaning the fact that his lodgings were costing him a shilling a night and asking his wife for a prompt response to his requests in view of the expense.

A response was obviously not forthcoming, since Edward appeared at the Brunswick Laundry and confronted Esther as she left work at eight o'clock that evening. The couple argued and Edward threatened Esther with the words 'You have seen this Easter but you will never see another.' When they parted company, Edward went straight to the pub, where he consumed several glasses of beer. He asked the pub landlord for a pencil and paper and sat at the bar writing for some time, eventually folding the paper up and putting it into his jacket pocket.

Having spent the night at his lodgings, Edward waited until four o'clock the next afternoon to knock on his father-in-law's door and ask to see his wife. The door was opened by Esther's brother, fifteen-year-old William Harding Hickley. 'Is Esther home?' Edward asked his brother-in-law, who invited him into the house and then went to tell his sister that she had a visitor.

Esther was in the back room of the house with her father and Arthur, who had measles. She asked her brother to show Edward in. Edward politely greeted his father-in-law and then lifted Arthur into his arms.

'I've got measles,' Arthur told him, at which Edward laughed and reassured him, 'It don't matter if your father do catch it.'

Edward was offered a seat and took a chair by the fire opposite his wife, asking her politely, 'Can I have five minutes' conversation with you?'

'Say what you've got to say here,' Esther told him.

George Hickley decided to give his daughter and son-in-law some privacy and left the room at this point, going out into the back garden, while William returned to reading his book at the back of the room.

'Is this affair going to come to an end?' asked Edward.

William didn't hear his sister's reply but before long Esther and Edward were arguing about money. Embarrassed, William tried to blot out their conversation and concentrate on his book. He was focusing intently on the pages when Watts suddenly shouted, 'Take that!' and the sound of a shot rang out.

Little Arthur fled from the room in terror, with William hot on his heels. As he ran out of the house, William heard three or four more shots fired in quick succession.

While William rushed frantically from street to street looking for a policeman, Mr Hickley heard the disturbance and hurried back into the house. His other son-in-law, William Lancaster, had got there before him and was now in possession of the revolver, with which Edward Watts had just shot his wife before turning the gun on himself. But while Esther Watts slumped back in her chair, blood gushing from her throat, her husband had somehow only managed to shoot himself through his left wrist, the bullet passing right through his arm, narrowly missing his artery.

Having shot Esther, Edward Watts calmly surrendered his gun to his brother-in-law and settled down to await the arrival of the police. 'She was too good for me,' he told his father and brother-in-law. 'She would never have lived with me and I could not ask her to forgive me again.'

When William Hickley returned with two policemen – brothers Stephen and Thomas Dorey – Watts assured them that he would go quietly, asking the policemen not to handcuff him. However, Stephen Dorey ignored his request and, having bound up his bleeding wrist with a handkerchief, escorted him to Buckland police station, where he handed him into the custody of Sergeant Hayward. Hayward arranged for surgeon Dr J. McGregor to treat his prisoner's wound and, having judged it to be a relatively minor injury, McGregor cleaned and bandaged it and gave Watts a sling to support his arm.

Meanwhile, Dr Josiah George Blackman had been urgently summoned to the Hickleys' home to attend to Esther. Sadly, she was dead by the time he arrived and, when he later conducted a post-mortem examination, he found that she had been shot several times.

A bullet had entered Esther's right wrist and exited through the base of her thumb, fracturing the bone. A second bullet had entered her chest, roughly two and a half inches above her right nipple. This bullet remained lodged in her body. There was a further bullet wound in the middle of her throat, with a corresponding exit wound at the side of her neck. A final bullet had been fired into her head at very close range, just behind her left ear. This had severed her spinal cord and splintered one of her vertebrae before exiting just behind her right ear and was, in Blackman's opinion, the wound which had ultimately proved fatal.

At an inquest into Esther's death, opened at the Town Hall by coroner Mr T.A. Bramsdon, it emerged that Watts had purchased the revolver on 28 March, just days before using it to shoot his wife. Receipts found in his pocket showed that, having made a down payment of just one shilling, he had been allowed to take the gun away from the shop, having agreed to pay the outstanding balance by instalments. In returning a verdict of wilful murder against Watts, the foreman of the coroner's jury stated that they wished to protest most strongly about the ease with which Watts had been able to procure a weapon, urging the government to bring about a licensing system for the purchase of guns and to establish a register of all gun owners.

Watts appeared before Mr Justice Cave at the Winchester Assizes in August 1891. While Mr Temple Cooke and Mr Rubie prepared to prosecute the case, the start of the trial was delayed for some time due to the late arrival of the train from London bearing barrister Mr Black, who had been engaged to act as defence counsel. Finally, the train arrived one hour late and Mr Temple Cooke was able to open the proceedings by describing the relationship between Edward and Esther Watts and the events leading up to the shooting.

The prosecution called several witnesses and, from his cross-examination of these witnesses, it quickly became evident that Mr Black was intending to rely on an insanity defence. He belaboured the point that Watts had twice suffered from severe sunstroke while serving in India with the army, after which his manner had been so eccentric that it amounted to insanity. Black's intentions backfired, as witness after witness called by the prosecution stated that they had never regarded Watts's behaviour as being in the slightest bit strange, apart from such strangeness as could be attributed to drunkenness.

It was only when Watts' mother, Mrs Blundell, took the stand that Black's line of questioning began to bear fruit. Called by the prosecution because she possessed some letters written by her son, Mrs Blundell told a sorry tale under cross-examination by her son's defence counsel.

According to Mrs Blundell, Watts had suffered two very severe bouts of sunstroke, which had made him more susceptible to alcohol, turning him 'quite mad' after drinking only a small amount. As a young baby, Watts had suffered from typhoid and, during the course of that illness had actually been pronounced dead three times. Mrs Blundell described her own brother as a 'perfect maniac', telling the court that he had once thrown Edward downstairs and injured his spine.

Watts's mother went on to say that she was herself prone to fits in her youth, during which she had 'lost her reason' for spells of seven or eight hours and done odd things, such as setting fire to the curtains. After recovering from the fits, she had no recollection of what she had done.

Town Hall, Portsmouth, 1905. (Author's collection)

Asked specifically about her son by Black, Mrs Blundell told the court that, whenever he was separated from his wife, he complained of severe pains in his head and his behaviour was 'strange' for periods of two or three days. His despair when Esther left him had led him to drink spirits, to which he was particularly susceptible. On two occasions, Mrs Blundell said that she had prevented her son from committing suicide, once when he was intending to take arsenic and a second time when he tried to shoot himself.

Mr Temple Cooke then gave his closing speech in which he pointed out to the jury that, with the sole exception of Mrs Blundell, nobody had regarded Edward Watts as anything but completely sane. On the afternoon of the murder, everyone who had encountered Watts had agreed that he was perfectly sober. There was 'not a tittle of evidence' to indicate that he was under the influence of alcohol when he shot his wife or that he was in the slightest bit insane.

Mr Black had little to offer in the way of defence for his client. He could not deny that Esther Watts had met her death at the hands of her husband but asked the jury to consider what their verdict might have been if there had been one more bullet in the gun or if Watts had succeeded in hitting a vital part of his body rather than just his wrist when he shot himself.

Had Watts been successful in his suicide attempt after the murder, a coroner's jury would doubtless have found that he had killed his wife and then himself while of unsound mind. Black argued that it therefore stood to reason that the jury should find that he was of unsound mind when he shot Esther. Black reminded the jury that numerous people had testified to the fact that the defendant was an exemplary son, husband and father and that his letters produced in court were full of husbandly affection. Indeed, the complete absence of any motive for the murder was yet another indication of the insanity of the accused, maintained Black.

It was left to Mr Justice Cave to summarise the evidence for the jury. Cave first pointed out that sunstroke was a long way from insanity and that, while it may have made the defendant more susceptible to the effects of alcohol, none of his associates had ever viewed him as a person of unsound mind. With the exception of his mother, everyone had treated him as a sane person – nobody had ever suspected that he might be delusional or become dangerous. Admittedly, he had been somewhat excitable when under the influence of drink, but that applied to a lot of people and was no excuse for murder.

With that, the jury retired to begin their deliberations. Edward Watts sat calmly in the dock, while Mr Justice Cave amused himself by playing with the murder weapon, repeatedly snapping the lock on and off. When the jury returned after about fifteen minutes, it was to pronounce Edward Henry Fawcett Watts 'Guilty' of the wilful murder of his wife.

Asked if he had anything to say why judgement of death should not be passed on him, Watts merely corrected the testimony of one of the witnesses with regard to the date of the assault of his wife in London. He added that his wife's mind had been poisoned against him by a woman he named as Mrs Fawcett. 'I am the victim of a terrible infatuation,' he concluded.

Taken to the condemned cell at Winchester Prison having been sentenced to death, Watts briefly lost the composure he had exhibited throughout his trial, weeping and beseeching God to sustain him in this his hour of need. Then, as if somehow ashamed of his emotions, he pulled himself together and calmly – even eagerly – awaited his appointment with executioner James Berry.

Watts laid the blame for the murder squarely on what he referred to as 'the demon drink'. He told Revd J. Ladbrooke, the prison chaplain, that he had made strenuous efforts to give up his addiction to alcohol and had once even signed the pledge. However, his workmates had teased him about his abstinence and he had foolishly allowed their chaffing to drive him from his teetotalism.

The *Hampshire Telegraph and Sussex Chronicle* describes Watt's last days in great detail, making much of the fact that, since he was considered a suicide risk, he was under constant watch. Four men – two of them old age pensioners – were employed to take shifts, watching Watts in pairs for twelve hours, day and night. In addition, the prisoner was not permitted the use of a razor and the neat moustache he customarily sported gradually grew into a bushy black beard, tinged with faint streaks of grey.

Watts walked steadily to the scaffold on 25 August 1891, having accepted his fate and made his peace with God. Only those closest to him noticed his terrified expression and convulsive trembling, although the newspaper reported that he did not suffer for long since it took less than three minutes for Berry to 'launch him into eternity'.

Note: In some contemporary newspaper accounts of the murder Edward Henry Fawcett Watts is alternatively named Henry Edward Fawcett Watts and, on one occasion, George Henry Fawcett Watts. Fawcett is also sometimes recorded as Faucett. William Hickley's age is variously given as fourteen, fifteen and sixteen years old.

17

'HURRY ALONG OR WE SHALL BE LATE HOME'

Southsea, 1893

It was every parent's worst nightmare. On 23 April 1893, five-year-old Emma Downton returned from Sunday school and asked to go out to play with her sister and brothers, Harriet, aged eleven, Willie, aged nine and three-year-old Edmund. At a quarter-past four in the afternoon, Mrs Harriet Downton watched her daughter walk along Garnier Street, Fratton. As the child turned the corner into Fratton Road, she disappeared – not just from her mother's view but apparently from the face of the earth.

When Emma didn't return home, her worried parents contacted the police, who immediately deployed every available officer to search for the missing child. They appealed for help through the press and details of Emma's disappearance took a prominent place in every newspaper in the Portsmouth area and beyond:

> Missing from her home, No. 72 Garnier Street, Fratton since 4.15 p.m. on the 23rd inst. Emma Downton, five years of age, about 2ft 6in. in height, long light hair down back, tied with cardinal coloured ribbon, dark blue eyes, fair complexion, stoutish build, round features, lisps when speaking, sore mark on left arm below elbow. Dress: White flannel chemise, no sleeves, but shoulder straps made with tape, herring bone stitch round neck and bottom, white calico chemise, lace edging round neck and sleeves (hand-made), red stays tied with strings, with white bone buttons thereon to fasten drawers, red twill button-up knicker drawers, with red embroidery and one tuck round each leg, white flannel petticoat with white calico band, tape strings, plain deep hem at bottom, one pink and white striped flannelette petticoat with calico bodice, tape shoulder straps, cardinal coloured frock, puff sleeves, kilted at bottom, with a deep piece of white lace round neck, fastens down back with cardinal coloured bone buttons, buff colour print pinafore, spray flower pattern, trimmed round neck and sleeves with cream embroidery, gathered at waist and tied at back with strings, black three-quarter socks, ribbed at top, button boots, rather worn at soles, have been half-soled and heeled, crushed strawberry-coloured plush bonnet (Mother Hubbard shape), pink silk front trimmed round edge with fawn coloured trimming similar to astrachan [*sic*] with satin strings to match bonnet. Please cause every possible enquiry to be made for this child and, if any trace can be obtained, wire Chief Constable Cosser, Police Department, Town Hall, Portsmouth.

Fratton Road, Southsea, 1907. (Author's collection)

Aided by members of the public, the police searched high and low for Emma but found no trace of the little girl, or indeed, any sightings of her after she left her home. Then, on the Tuesday following her disappearance, they finally received an important clue. A Mrs Urry of Alver Road, Kingston, which was situated just a short walk from Emma's home, visited the Buckland police station, bearing some scraps of material. When Emma's mother was shown the scraps, she was immediately able to identify them as having come from her daughter's bonnet.

Mrs Urry explained that her fourteen-year-old daughter, Elizabeth Ada Urry (aka Elizabeth Whiting), had found the bonnet lying between two boats on the beach at Southsea at about five o'clock on the previous Sunday evening. Having asked a few bystanders if they owned the bonnet, Elizabeth eventually brought it home with her and cut it up intending to make some dolls' clothes for her little sister. When the police spoke to Elizabeth, she also produced a length of cardinal red ribbon, identical to the one that Mrs Downton had used to tie back Emma's hair, which she said she had found on the beach at the same time as the bonnet.

The police had already searched empty houses, outbuildings, yards, wasteland and every other place where a child might either hide or be hidden. Now the focus of the search switched to the beach at Southsea and the sea was dragged in the hope of finding the missing child or more items of her clothing. The search proved fruitless. The police were unable to find any trace of Emma and, initially, neither could they find any witnesses who had seen her or Elizabeth Urry at the beach that afternoon.

Elizabeth told them that she had been taking a neighbour's child out for an airing in its pram. However, when the police questioned Mrs Waters, the mother of three-year-old Dolly, with whom Elizabeth had been entrusted, they were told that Elizabeth had kept the child out far later than she was supposed to have done. Furthermore, on bringing

Dolly home, she had simply abandoned her pram at the door of the Waters' house in Fratton road at nine o'clock at night and run away, before Mrs Waters got the chance to remonstrate with her about keeping her daughter out so late.

The police also spoke to a little girl, Helena Elizabeth Jane Langridge, who happened to be at Mrs Urry's home when Elizabeth returned that night. Helena told the police that the bonnet was already cut into pieces when Elizabeth took it out of her pocket.

As the police continued to publicise their search for missing Emma, witnesses came forward to say that they had seen Elizabeth Urry pushing a child in a pram close to the Downtons' home at 4.20 p.m. on the afternoon of 23 April. Later that afternoon, Elizabeth was seen again at Fratton Bridge, still pushing the pram, but now with a little girl who matched Emma's description walking beside her. Thus, what appeared to be the last confirmed sighting of Emma Downton placed her with Elizabeth Urry and the police decided that Elizabeth should be brought in for further questioning.

A warrant was obtained for her arrest and, on 29 April, Detective Sergeant Money called at Elizabeth Urry's home and took her by cab to the Town Hall. She appeared before magistrates on the following Monday morning and was remanded in custody for a week to allow the police more time in which to question her.

Elizabeth continued to deny any knowledge of the whereabouts of Emma Downton until the Tuesday morning, when she finally made a statement. Accompanied by Mr Hobbs, a solicitor who had been retained to act for Elizabeth, the police immediately rushed to a building site near to the Highland Road Cemetery in Southsea. There they found a well, which was approximately nineteen feet deep and had about six feet of water at the bottom. Detective Taylor was lowered by rope to the bottom of the well, where he dragged the water using a hook borrowed from the builders on the site. When the hook snagged something in the depths of the water, the police realised that their search for Emma Downton was not to have a happy ending.

Elizabeth Ada Urry.

An inquest was opened on 5 May by Portsmouth coroner Mr T.A. Bramsdon. Although the coroner did not initially go into too much medical detail, he produced a gasp of horror from all those assembled in the Police Court when he revealed that the preliminary findings of the post-mortem examination on Emma Downton showed that she had not drowned in the well but had been strangled by a handkerchief tied tightly around her neck.

By now, the police had traced several more witnesses who had seen Elizabeth Urry on the afternoon of 23 April, either alone with Dolly Waters in her pram or with a child matching Emma's description walking beside her. Among these was a Mrs Lydia Wise, who had seen Elizabeth at Lump's Fort and had spoken to her sharply, as the pram containing little Dolly seemed to be in imminent danger of falling off the sea wall into the sea. Mrs Wise told the inquest that Emma seemed to be very tired, so much so that she was actually swaying. Mrs Wise told Elizabeth to be careful that the little girl didn't fall over. Elizabeth didn't reply but chided Emma to walk faster, saying, 'Hurry along or we shall be late home.' Mrs Wise told the inquest that Emma had looked at her 'so pitifully' but had not spoken.

The last confirmed sighting of Emma Downton now appeared to have been made by lamp lighter Mr Joseph Loveridge, who had seen the little girl walking with Elizabeth and the pram in Lawrence Road at about 7.40 p.m. At the time, Loveridge was particularly struck by the fact that Emma wasn't wearing a jacket and wondered whether she might be cold.

As well as those who had seen Elizabeth with the two children, two witnesses came forward to say that they had seen the little group in the company of a soldier. One witness stated that the soldier had been wearing the uniform of the Royal Artillery.

While in custody at Kingston Prison, Elizabeth Urry made a statement to the governor, Edward Simpson, in the presence of her solicitor, Mr Hobbs, and the prison matron, Ellen Worman. In her statement, which was transcribed by clerk Mr Bleach and later signed by Elizabeth, she related that she had been out walking with Dolly Waters in her pram on 23 April when she had come across Emma Downton crying in the street. She asked Emma what the matter was and the little girl sobbed that she wanted her sister. Elizabeth told her that she would try and find her and asked her to hold on to the pram handle. They had walked as far as Clarence Pier on Southsea beach, where they had spent some time playing. At this time, she had spoken to a soldier who was sleeping on a bench and had woken up when Elizabeth and the children approached.

Emma had needed to go to the toilet, so Elizabeth took her to a pub and asked permission to use the toilet there. She later complained of feeling cold, so Elizabeth wrapped a handkerchief around her throat in an effort to warm her. Realising that they were not going to find Emma's sister, Elizabeth decided to take the child home, so they walked across the common, eventually reaching the Albert Road Bridge. At this point, Elizabeth suddenly realised that Emma was no longer with her. She searched but was unable to find her. During her search, Elizabeth noticed the well, which she said was covered with a piece of corrugated iron and had an opening large enough for a child to fall through. Realising that she had lost the child, Elizabeth had become frightened that she would be blamed for her disappearance and had told nobody that she had seen the child that afternoon.

Once Elizabeth's statement had been admitted as evidence, the coroner adjourned the inquest at the request of the Public Prosecutor, to allow the police more time to conclude their investigations.

Clarence pier and promenade, Southsea, 1920s. (Author's collection)

Clarence pier and beach, 1920s. (Author's collection)

The inquest was resumed on 12 May. Mrs Elizabeth Urry senior was the first person to give evidence, telling the inquest that she had given her daughter a telling-off on the night of 23 April for staying out so late with young Dolly. Shown the handkerchief that had been tied around Emma Downton's neck, Mrs Urry said that she didn't know if it belonged to her daughter or not.

The next witnesses were a labourer and a watchman, working at the site of the well, who told the inquest that it was covered with a sheet of corrugated iron weighing 28lb and that it was impossible for a child to fall down it accidentally unless the cover was removed.

The inquest then heard from Dr Lysander Maybury, the police surgeon who had initially examined Emma's body and later conducted the post-mortem examination. Maybury assured the inquest that Emma had been strangled with a calico handkerchief, tied tightly around her neck and secured with a granny knot. He was certain that Emma had not died from drowning and that she had been dead before entering the well. When Maybury had given his evidence, the inquest was adjourned for a second time.

When the inquest resumed, Maybury was recalled and asked about the length of time it would have taken Emma Downton to die. He gave his opinion that, to kill her, once the handkerchief had been tightened around her neck, the pressure would need to be maintained consistently for between four and five minutes. The coroner's jury were understandably very anxious to know if it would have been possible for the strangulation to have been accidental, but Maybury was quick to assure them that this was practically impossible. Furthermore, he had since conducted some experiments with similar handkerchiefs, to see if they would shrink when immersed in water. They had not shrunk at all, leading Maybury to conclude that the action of the water in the well had not caused the handkerchief to tighten around the child's neck. Maybury's evidence was corroborated by Dr John Robert Stephenson Robertson, who had assisted him in conducting the post-mortem examination.

The coroner then summed up the evidence for his jury. Advising them to disregard any statements about a soldier, he asked them to look at the evidence carefully and to consider several questions; was strangulation the cause of Emma Downton's death? If so, by who was she strangled and was the strangulation wilful and intentional? If it was not wilful and intentional, was it accidental or the result of culpable negligence or carelessness?

After retiring for twenty-seven minutes, the jury returned to say that fourteen of the fifteen members were agreed on a verdict. They believed that Emma Downton had been wilfully strangled by Elizabeth Urry.

Elizabeth Urry was committed for trial at the next assizes on a coroner's warrant. At a special sitting of the magistrates' court, the charge against her was upgraded from one of enticing away Emma Downton to one of wilful murder. (She was charged under the name of Elizabeth Whiting.)

The trial opened before Mr Justice Day on 5 July 1893, with Mr Bucknill QC and Mr Folkard prosecuting and Mr Charles Mathews defending. Although both prosecuting counsels were amongst the most experienced in the country at the time, a meeting was called between the defence and the prosecution before the start of the trial, at which Mr Mathews suggested to the prosecution that there was a 'missing link' in the chain of evidence against his client which, in his opinion, would make it impossible for any jury to convict her of wilful murder. The 'missing link' referred to was the complete absence of any apparent motive for the killing of Emma Downton by Elizabeth Whiting, without which it was impossible for the prosecution to show that the defendant had any 'wicked feeling' towards the deceased.

Mr Justice Day remarked that it was not for him to pass judgement on the weight of evidence available for the prosecution but he conceded that, in the absence of proof by the prosecution that the defendant had wilfully murdered Emma Downton, he would need to instruct the jury on the possibility of a manslaughter verdict. If Mr Bucknill believed that, with the evidence he had at his disposal, there was a probability that the jury might return a verdict on a charge of wilful murder then Day felt it was his duty to proceed with the trial.

Mr Mathews, for the defence, then laid his cards on the table, offering a plea of guilty by his client to the lesser charge of manslaughter.

'Your lordship, if I understand your remarks rightly, if I believed a verdict of wilful murder could not be found, I might adopt the course suggested by Mr Mathews?' asked Mr Bucknill, seeking legal clarification on the matter in question.

'I think you can take a plea of manslaughter if you think, upon your knowledge of the evidence, that a verdict of wilful murder would not be found,' responded the judge.
With that, Mr Bucknill agreed to accept a plea of guilty of manslaughter from the defendant. Mr Mathews turned to Elizabeth Whiting in the dock and advised her to withdraw her plea of not guilty to the charge of wilful murder and plead guilty to the alternative charge of manslaughter. After much prompting and coaxing from her counsel, the tearful fourteen-year-old eventually complied.

This action negated the need for a trial by jury and it remained only for the judge to determine an appropriate sentence. Mr Mathews spoke on behalf of his client, painting a picture of Emma as a tired little girl, who was complaining about the cold. Pointing out that Elizabeth had always previously shown a great fondness for children, Mathews suggested that she had placed the handkerchief around the child's neck to try and keep her warm. Then, having difficult in getting the tired child to keep up with her, and being exhausted herself, Mathews suggested that Elizabeth might have unwittingly pulled on the handkerchief to encourage Emma to keep moving.

Mathews pointed out that the medical evidence suggested that death was due to suffocation rather than strangulation and that there were no marks of violence on Emma Downton's body. While conceding that taking the child away in the first place was an illegal act, he suggested that the child's death had been both instantaneous and inadvertent. He admitted that Elizabeth had then concealed Emma's body and that she had subsequently told many lies about her involvement with the child but maintained that this was because she was frightened and had sought to conceal Emma's whereabouts out of fear of the consequences of the child dying while in her company. He requested that, in view of Elizabeth's tender age and previous good character, the judge should treat her as leniently as possible.

Mathews then called a series of character witnesses, all of whom made a point of emphasising Elizabeth's love of children. Mr Bucknill then asked for Dr Maybury to be recalled but Maybury had already left.

Saying that he would like to consult with the doctor before deciding on his sentence, Mr Justice Day adjourned the proceedings until Maybury could be recalled. Then, after having a private word with the doctor, the judge decided on his sentence.

Addressing the defendant, the judge told her that the main difficulty he had faced when determining an appropriate sentence was her extreme youth. While he did not wish to comment in great details about the circumstances of the case, Mr Justice Day said that he was in no doubt that Elizabeth had 'inveigled or decoyed' Emma Downton into following her and that the 'poor little child' had subsequently met her death at Elizabeth's hands. Had Elizabeth been an adult, said Day, in view of her plea of 'Guilty' to the charge of manslaughter, he would have had no hesitation whatsoever in meting out the harshest possible sentence open to him. As it was, Day admitted to struggling to find the right balance in order to discharge his duty to the public. He therefore felt that Elizabeth's sentence should be imprisonment and thus, in view of her age, he was sentencing her to five years penal servitude.

Elizabeth Whiting left the dock in tears to start her sentence. As the *Hampshire Telegraph and Sussex Chronicle* were quick to point out in their report of the trial, the verdict and sentence came as quite a surprise to many people in view of the fact that the Grand Jury had found a true bill for wilful murder and that the accused had been committed for trial for that offence on a coroner's warrant. Apart from that, two of the country's most experienced and capable counsels had been engaged to prosecute the case. Provided that Elizabeth Whiting behaved herself, she could expect to be released on a ticket of leave within three years, when she would still be only around eighteen years old. The sentence of grief for Emma Downton's parents would last a lifetime.

18

'THAT WILL BE THE LAST CUP OF TEA YOU SHALL FLING AT ME'

Binsted, 1894

In 1894, George Chappell was the landlord of the Cricketers Inn at Binsted in name only. Having reached the ripe old age of ninety-four, and growing ever frailer by the day, Chappell had handed over the day-to-day running of the pub to his daughter, Frances Knight, and her husband, Cyrus. As well as helping out in the pub, Cyrus Knight also worked as a hire carter, although it seemed that he spent a large proportion of his earnings on drink.

On 28 September, William Brewer – the Knights' fifteen-year-old adopted son – arrived home from work at about half-past seven in the evening. He sat at the kitchen table to eat his tea and Frances went to fetch Cyrus, who was enjoying a drink and a game of dominoes in the pub.

Cyrus made sure that he finished his game before going to eat his supper and, when he sat down at the table, his wife immediately began to give him a thorough ticking off for stopping and drinking at public houses while he was at his carting work. Cyrus simply ignored her, reaching for the milk jug and emptying it into his teacup.

Exasperated, Frances snatched the cup from him and poured some of the milk into her own cup and some into William's. Still without speaking, Cyrus retrieved his cup and threw its contents at his wife, hitting the front of her dress. Frances promptly threw the contents of her cup at her husband, soaking his waistcoat, and Cyrus retaliated by throwing his empty cup at her. The cup bounced off Frances and shattered on the floor.

Only then did Cyrus speak. Standing up from the table he turned to his wife and said menacingly, 'That will be the last cup of tea you shall fling at me.' And, with those parting words, he picked up his jacket and abruptly left the room.

He returned within minutes, a gun in his right hand and, without speaking, crossed the kitchen and marched out through the back door into the garden, pulling the door almost closed as he left. Minutes later, William spotted the muzzle of the gun poking through the kitchen door, aimed directly at his mother, who was by now washing up the tea things at the kitchen sink. The shotgun was fired twice in quick succession and Frances Knight immediately fell to the floor, blood pumping from a wound in her throat.

William screamed in horror and ran out into the bar of the pub for help. There he found Jim Sampson Light, a gypsy who had been living in a caravan in a field attached to the pub for almost two months while hop picking. Hearing William's frantic shout of 'Jim, Jim – father's shot mother,' Light jumped to his feet and followed the boy back into the kitchen but he quickly realised that Frances Knight was beyond all assistance, so went to fetch a doctor and the police. Meanwhile, Cyrus had disappeared into the night, leaving the shotgun propped up against the door of his neighbour's cottage.

Surgeon William Kay arrived from Bentley at about ten o'clock and found Frances lying on her back, in a large pool of coagulating blood. Having pronounced her dead, her body was left to await the arrival of the police from nearby Alton.

The police arrived early the following morning and were in the process of searching the kitchen when Cyrus Knight returned to the pub. Inspector Hawkins immediately arrested him on suspicion of the wilful murder of his wife. 'I couldn't help it,' Knight said. 'The gun went off accidentally.' Knight then asked to see Frances for the last time and Inspector Hawkins allowed him to look at her body. According to Hawkins, Cyrus seemed 'only a little affected' when viewing the body, any emotions he might have felt betrayed by no more than a little trembling.

Dr Kay conducted a post-mortem examination on the body of Frances Knight, pronouncing her an otherwise healthy fifty-three-year-old woman who had died as a result of blood loss from a shotgun wound to her neck, just below her jaw on the left-hand side. He removed shot, wadding and a small piece of wire from the wound.

The inquest into Frances Knight's death was held in one of the bedrooms at the Cricketer's Arms before county coroner Mr H. White. The local paper, the *Hampshire Chronicle*, wrote:

> The charm of a lovely autumn day heightening the beauties of nature so generously bestowed around and with nothing outwardly to disturb the peaceful hush of rural life, it was a wrench to one's feelings to remember the why and the wherefore men had come together. And as the miserable story, with its touches of pathos and home, was unfolded in the presence of the wretched accused – worn and dejected – it all seemed terribly sorrowful.

The coroner's jury first heard from William Brewer, who found himself in an unenviable position. Although Frances had originally adopted William while she was married to her late first husband, since she had married Cyrus in 1887, William had come to think of him as a father and was now obviously reluctant to testify against him. Both Brewer and a neighbour, Harriet Collins, who lived in a cottage attached to the pub, told the inquest that Frances and Cyrus were usually on good terms but that, when drunk, Cyrus Knight became a different person. Normally a quiet man, the effects of drink turned him into a violent, vindictive bully and, on previous occasions, he had not only hit Frances but also threatened to kill her. Cyrus, who was present at the inquest at his own request, seemed bemused and denied these allegations, saying, 'I don't know as how I ever threatened my wife,' adding when questioned by the coroner, 'I have never threatened her in my life that I know of.'

Jim Sampson Light told the inquest that the gun was one that he had given to Cyrus Knight two months earlier to sell for him. Cyrus had kept the gun while waiting to find a buyer, although Light had used it on occasions to shoot rabbits. All the witnesses who had been present at the Cricketers Arms on the night of the shooting described Cyrus Knight as having been under the influence of liquor at the time, although not drunk.

Cyrus himself gave a statement at the inquest. After some discussion as to whether or not he should be formally sworn, he told the coroner that he had intended to take the gun out that night to do some shooting. He had carried the gun out of the kitchen propped on his right arm, but had moved it to his left arm, intending to shut the kitchen door behind him with his right hand. As he went to close the door, Cyrus maintained that the gun had gone off accidentally. He heard his wife say, 'I'm shot,' and immediately put the gun down and left – he didn't remember where he had been all night.

The coroner then summed up the evidence for the jury, reminding them that, when sober, Knight was a quiet, harmless man who seemed to 'break out' under the influence of drink. Mr White stressed to the jury that drink was no excuse for crime. He also pointed out that nobody had actually seen Cyrus Knight firing the shots that killed his wife but, from the evidence presented at the inquest, the inference was that it had been he who had fired the fatal shots. In fact, Knight himself admitted it, although he would have the inquest believe that the shooting was accidental.

Having deliberated for a short while, the jury asked if they might see the kitchen where the shooting took place. Their request was granted and, having been escorted downstairs, they quickly returned a verdict of wilful murder against Cyrus Knight. Somewhat surprisingly, a crowd of people had assembled outside the pub and, when Knight was taken from the inquest to be detained while awaiting his trial, the crowd seemed keen to wish him well. Many even tried to shake his hand, but were prevented from doing so by the attendant police officers.

After a hearing at Alton Magistrates' Court, Cyrus Knight was committed to the next Hampshire Assizes to stand trial. The proceedings opened on 16 November under Sir William Grantham, with Mr Blake Odgers prosecuting and Mr Bullen defending.

The trial began with an account of the inquest, which immediately spawned a discussion about the truth of Knight's remark that he had heard his wife say 'I'm shot'. Dr Kay told the court that such were the extent of Frances Knight's injuries that she would have been unable to speak.

Mr Bullen found himself with a difficult task in defending the accused. The only living witness, William Brewer, had been called by the prosecution, hence all Bullen could offer was a defence of accidental death, as his client continued to insist the shooting was.

Mr Bullen stated that there had been some variation in William Brewer's accounts of the actual words spoken by Cyrus Knight after Frances had thrown the dregs of her tea at him. There was, Bullen pointed out, a vast difference between the words 'That will be the last cup of tea you shall fling at me' and 'You shall not throw any more tea at me', both of which phrases had been quoted by William Brewer at various stages of the enquiry. Bullen told the jury that the exact words spoken by Cyrus Knight were uncertain and that the second phrase did not imply any threat towards Frances.

Although Knight was undoubtedly under the influence of drink, he was not so drunk that he couldn't differentiate between right and wrong. If, as had been suggested, Knight was so incensed at his wife that he wanted to kill her, why had he not shot her immediately rather than walking outside and waiting for a few minutes before doing so?

Bullen demonstrated Knight's actions to the court, showing how the gun could have been accidentally discharged as he moved it from one arm to the other in order to close the door. He asked why William had not shouted a warning to his mother when he had seen the gun and finally asked them if they believed that Cyrus Knight's life should rest on the evidence of a fifteen-year-old boy who had repeatedly changed his evidence at the inquest, magistrates' court and also at the assizes.

It was left to the judge to sum up the case. He began by musing that he could not recall a murder case in which there was so little evidence and that the prosecution's case was largely reliant on evidence of previous ill-feeling between the accused and his wife. However, in the judge's opinion, that evidence was less relevant that it would have been had the charge against Knight been one of manslaughter. All that could be said was that Knight had used unkind words and bad language while under the influence of drink and maybe even hit his wife once or twice – other than that he had been a good husband.

Sir William Grantham then turned to the mechanics of the gun, telling the jury that Knight could simply have ejected the cartridges rather than firing the gun had he simply wanted to get rid of the bullets. The court had heard from a gunsmith, Mr Smith, who had stated that, in his opinion, it would have been impossible to discharge the gun accidentally and the judge agreed, adding that the act of running away after the shots had been fired did not sit well with the explanation of the gun being fired accidentally. Surely anyone who had accidentally fired a gun would at least have stopped to see whether or not he had caused any harm?

The jury deliberated for less than ten minutes before returning their verdict. The foreman stated that the jury found Knight guilty of shooting his wife during a fit of temper, but strongly recommended mercy. 'Do you find him guilty of murder?' asked the clerk of the court, to which the foreman replied, 'Of wilfully shooting her.' Judge Grantham eventually intervened in the rather confused exchange, asking the foreman if he meant that the jury found the prisoner guilty of wilful murder with a strong recommendation for mercy.

The jury agreed that that was exactly what they meant and the judge, stating that he agreed with their verdict, sentenced Cyrus Knight to death. The jury's recommendations for mercy obviously came to nothing as forty-five-year-old Cyrus Knight was duly hanged by James Billington at Winchester on 12 December 1894.

19

'PROMISE YOU'LL BE GOOD TO HER'

Copnor, 1896

At about eight o'clock on the morning of 7 April 1896, labourer William Barber found the body of a little girl in a potato field at Baffin's Farm, Copnor, near Portsmouth. The pretty, fair-haired child, who was approximately five years old, was well nourished and respectably dressed and Barber's first thought was that she was sleeping peacefully, her head resting on a pile of clothes and a sheet of brown paper draped over her legs like a blanket. It was only when Barber got closer to the little girl and gently touched her face that he realised that she was dead.

Barber felt the child's chest for a heartbeat and, not finding one, hastened to summon the police and a doctor. PC Penfold, the first officer to arrive, arranged for the little girl's body to be transported to the mortuary. There, she was examined by police surgeon Dr Lysander Maybury at 11.15 a.m., at which time her body was still warm, although her limbs were cold to the touch and the doctor estimated that she had died between six and twenty-four hours prior to his examination. On the following day, Maybury conducted a post-mortem examination on the body, assisted by Dr James McGregor. The girl's face was swollen and red and her eyes were open and bulging. The doctors found that the child had three marks on her throat, which appeared to have been made by human fingers, from which they surmised that she had been manually throttled.

There was no sign of a struggle having taken place in the area where the body was found, although the ground was very hard and had been heavily trampled by workmen in the days prior to the discovery of the dead child. Close to her body lay a hairbrush marked 'Elsie' and a small piece of apple, as well as the bundle of clean clothes on which her head rested, some of which were marked with the name 'Piggott'. Surprisingly, considering that she had obviously been well cared for, there had been no recent reports of any missing children.

The police turned to the newspapers to publicise the tragic discovery and as soon as the child's description was published, they began to receive information from members of the public suggesting a name. On Thursday 9 April, two people viewed the child's body and both confirmed that she was Elsie Gertrude Matthews of Teignmouth, Devon.

Elsie's father, Philip Matthews, had served as a coachman to Dr Piggott, the medical officer of health for Teignmouth, and was highly regarded by his employer, who described

Above & below: *Teignmouth, Devon. (Both author's collection)*

him as hard working, trustworthy and honest. In October 1888, he married and, in June 1891, his wife, Elizabeth, gave birth to a little girl, who the couple named Elsie Gertrude. Tragically, Elizabeth Matthews died in February 1892 but Dr and Mrs Piggott took in baby Elsie and cared for her as if she were their own child.

In August of 1892, Matthews remarried and Elsie was returned to her father and stepmother, Maria. Both Philip and Maria were said to be very fond of the child but, shortly after their marriage, Dr Piggott rented some stables at the West Lawn Boarding Establishment on the Exeter Road, Teignmouth and Matthews, as his coachman, moved into the lodge house there to be close to the horses.

Before long, Charlotte Maloney, an attractive parlour maid at the boarding house, caught Philip's eye and the couple embarked on a clandestine affair. Charlotte expressed a desire to return to her native Portsmouth and when she left Teignmouth on 23 March 1896, Philip Matthews went with her, representing himself as Charlotte's husband.

Philip left little Elsie in Maria's care, although, after leaving his job, he was unable to support her financially and Maria was understandably unhappy about having been left literally 'holding the baby'. When Philip returned home on 2 April, cross words were exchanged between them and Philip agreed to make alternative arrangements for Elsie, telling Maria that he would be taking the child to London, where she would be well cared for.

Accordingly, Maria packed up Elsie's clothes in a brown paper parcel, along with a paper bag containing some chocolate and biscuits for the journey, which she gave to Philip when he finally came to collect the child on 6 April. Maria went to the station with her husband and stepdaughter and watched them board the 7.27 p.m. train to Exeter.

'Promise you'll be good to her,' Maria begged him and Philip assured her that he would, saying that he would write and let her know where Elsie was in due course. Maria received a telegram from her husband the next morning, which was the day on which Elsie's body was discovered in Copnor. The telegram was sent from Botley and read: 'Safe. London. Long letter. Tired. Phil.'

The promised long letter arrived the following day and was also addressed from Botley. Matthews wrote: 'I left Elsie looking so happy and hope I may see you happy. If prayers and good wishes can help you, I send you abundance' [sic]. Matthews continued by asking Maria not to think badly of Charlotte Maloney, admitting that he had led her on and that the girls in Teignmouth had ruined his good name. 'I cannot come back to you,' Philip's letter continued. 'I have only a few shillings given me by a friend.' Adding that he was asking 'the master' [Mr Piggott] to send him some money to come back with, the letter ended abruptly, although there was another piece of paper enclosed on which he had written:

Please pardon me. I know that you will do all you can for Elsie. Ask the doctor to do his best, which I am sure he will. May God help you in all your troubles. Those who know me from birth will be surprised. My last prayer is may you and Elsie be happy [sic].

Written across the scrap of paper was the word 'Goodbye'. Unbeknown to Maria Matthews, her husband had been in Portsmouth with Charlotte Maloney.

When Elsie's body was found, her description in the newspapers was recognised by both Charlotte Maloney and also by Mr Westcott, a greengrocer and lodging-house keeper from Teignmouth, with whom Maria and Elsie Matthews had been lodging since Philip Matthews abandoned them. Both Miss Maloney and Mr Westcott made the journey to the mortuary in Portsmouth, where they positively identified the child's body as that of little Elsie Matthews.

Once Elsie had been identified, the police immediately began a hunt for her father, dragging Saffin's Pond, near to where the child's body had been discovered, in case he had drowned himself there. When nothing was found, a telegram was sent to all police stations in the area by the Chief Constable of Portsmouth, advising them to be on the look-out for Matthews and, within ten minutes of receiving the telegram, the appropriately named Sergeant Luck made an arrest.

Having run short of money, Matthews sent a wire to some friends in Teignmouth asking for help. The Fareham postmaster, Mr Stedman, thought he fitted the description of the wanted man in the telegram from the Chief of Police and contacted the police to inform them that Matthews was staying at the Lamb Inn, Fareham. Within minutes of receiving the Chief Constable's telegram, Luck strolled down to the Lamb and arrested his suspect. On hearing that Matthews had been arrested, Detective Goff of Portsmouth was so keen to interview him that, arriving at Portsmouth station and finding that he had just missed the train, he set out to walk to Fareham via Gosport, rather than waiting for the next one.

Matthews denied having murdered his daughter. In his statement to the police, he told them that he had collected her from Teignmouth and travelled by train to Fratton station, arriving at about one o'clock in the morning. From there, he had intended to walk to Cosham but had lost his way in the darkness. As they neared Baffin's Farm, Matthews told Detective Goff that some dogs had begun barking, at which little Elsie had quite literally died of fright. Matthews said he hadn't known what to do. He placed his daughter's body near the hedge and went to the home of Charlotte Maloney's mother, arriving there at ten past four in the morning.

An inquest was opened into the death of Elsie Matthews by Portsmouth coroner Mr T.A. Bramsdon. The first witness was Joseph Westcott, who recalled Matthews collecting the child from her stepmother. Westcott stated that he had threatened Matthews, 'If anything happens to the child, I will fetch you back if it costs me a £10 note.'

Charlotte Maloney was the next to testify. Described as 'a tall, dark, stylishly-dressed young woman of extremely prepossessing appearance', she related meeting Philip Matthews in Teignmouth and being told that Elsie was the illegitimate child of Matthews' first wife. She and Matthews left Teignmouth together for Portsmouth, where, believing Matthews to be legally separated from his wife, she introduced him to her mother as her husband.

Matthews had then told her that he had received word from Maria saying that she was not prepared to keep Elsie any longer and was going to put her in the workhouse. Matthews left Portsmouth on 6 April, although he said nothing to Charlotte about fetching Elsie from her stepmother and either bringing her back to Portsmouth or placing her with friends. She had not seen him again until the morning of 7 April, when he was alone and appeared very agitated. He had not mentioned Elsie at the time and Charlotte had not heard from him since then.

After the inquest had heard from Charlotte Maloney's mother, Dr Maybury was called to give evidence on his findings at the post-mortem examination of Elsie's body. He told the inquest that the child had been manually strangled by someone using one hand to exert pressure on her throat. He denied the possibility that Elsie had died from fright, explaining that, had that been the case, her body would have had a completely different appearance. Her face would have been pale rather than suffused with blood, her brain would not have been congested and there would have been no finger marks on her neck.

Fratton railway station, 1908. (Author's collection)

After several adjournments, the coroner's jury eventually returned a verdict of wilful murder against Philip Matthews, who was committed for trial at the next assizes in Winchester. As a result of the publicity surrounding his case, an assistant in a jeweller's shop contacted the police alleging that Philip Matthews had stolen a gold and diamond ring from her shop on 1 April. However, since Matthews was currently awaiting his trial for a capital offence, there was little point in prosecuting him for theft.

The trial for wilful murder was headed by Mr Justice Day. Mr Temple Cooke and Mr H.W. McGee prosecuted the case for the Treasury and Mr W.M. Barnes defended Philip Matthews, who pleaded 'Not Guilty' to the charge against him.

The prosecution insisted that Matthews had killed his daughter because of his grave financial situation – he could not afford to keep her, as well as maintaining his first wife and a new wife, Charlotte Maloney. (There was also apparently yet another wife, whom Matthews had married in Leicestershire, although nobody was quite sure if she was dead or alive.)

In the days immediately prior to the murder, Matthews wrote several letters to Dr Piggott, which showed that he was desperately short of money and suggested that he was planning to commit suicide. Yet he had made desperate attempts to marry Charlotte, even though he was still legally married to Maria. The registrar of marriages at Exeter testified that, as early as 27 January, Matthews was making enquiries about the price of a marriage licence and the earliest possible day on which he could get married. On 23 March, Matthews applied for a special licence at Wilton, setting 25 March as the date for the wedding ceremony and, although he and Maloney had not actually married, they sent out marriage announcement cards to their friends.

Charlotte Maloney initially gave her evidence calmly, although she broke down and wept towards the end of her testimony. Having stated that she was pregnant, she was allowed a seat in the dock. She admitted to having been very fond of Elsie and was asked by the counsel for the prosecution if she would have had any objection to the little girl living with her and Matthews. 'It was never suggested to me,' she told the court, tearfully.

Several witnesses had made the same train journey as Matthews and his daughter and all testified that Matthews treated the little girl kindly, fetching her drinks of milk and gratefully accepting an apple that one of the other passengers gave him for Elsie.

Matthews stuck to his story that his daughter had died from fright and, although his defence counsel called no witnesses, he fought hard to suggest that Elsie's death had been a tragic accident that occurred when she was asleep in her father's arms in the field. Yet this theory didn't explain the finger marks on the child's neck, illustrated in court by enlarged photographs produced by Dr Maybury. Neither did it explain why an apparently loving father had not rushed to get help the instant he suspected that his daughter had died.

'Will you show us how it was done?' Mr Temple Cooke asked Maybury.

'I can hardly do it on my own throat. I could on somebody else's,' responded the doctor, provoking a ripple of laughter around the court room.

Detective Taylor stepped into the witness box and allowed Maybury to demonstrate precisely how he believed Elsie had been throttled. Mr Temple Cooke prompted him to repeat his demonstration, this time indicating how Elsie could have been killed if she had been lying on her father's left arm at the time.

According to Maybury, a child of Elsie's age was easily throttled and her killer would not need to have used a great deal of pressure. As he had done at the inquest, Maybury explained his findings at the post-mortem examination to the jury, with particular emphasis on what he would have expected to find had Elsie died of fright as her father insisted she had. When cross-examined by the defence, Maybury admitted that he had previously performed a post-mortem examination on a person who had actually died from fright and so knew from experience exactly what signs to look out for.

The medical evidence – which apparently negated Matthews' explanation – coupled with Maybury's re-enactment of the murder, ultimately proved most persuasive for the jury and, after retiring for just fifteen minutes, they returned a verdict of 'Guilty'. Charlotte Maloney immediately fainted.

Philip Matthews was described as 'a man of military bearing'. His grey eyes had twice filled briefly with tears – once at the very start of the trial and once more when he heard Maybury describing Elsie's death in great detail. He remained composed as the judge asked him if he had anything to say before sentence was passed.

'I am not guilty,' he insisted, adding, 'I am only sorry I cannot be allowed to explain where I was between four and ten o'clock.'

Mr Justice Day showed more emotion in pronouncing sentence of death than Matthews did on hearing the judge's words. 'I am glad to be going where my child is', Matthews said before being removed from the dock to the condemned cell at Winchester Prison. The contemporary newspapers reported that he spent most of his time there talking of love and women and writing love letters and poems to Charlotte Maloney. (The prison authorities were later to deny this, saying that talk of that description would not be encouraged.)

Nevertheless, Matthews seemed to draw great comfort from the belief that he would soon be with Elsie in heaven and, on 27 July 1896, he went willingly to the gallows where he was hanged together with two other convicted murderers, Frederick Burden and Samuel Smith.

Note: Elsie's age at the time of her murder is variously given as four, five, six and seven years old. The date of birth that I have used (June 1891) was taken from the Matthews family Bible, produced at the inquest by Maria Matthews, although some sources report the entry as reading July 1891 and official records of Elsie's death give her date of birth as 'about 1892'. During the trial, Dr Piggott testified to attending at the birth of Elsie on 29 July 1891. In addition, some contemporary newspapers state that Elsie was in fact the illegitimate daughter of Philip Matthews' first wife, Elizabeth and that she was born before their marriage. Again, I have taken the details as recorded in the Bible, although there is, of course, no guarantee that these are correct, or that they were accurately reported. Some newspapers record Elsie's father's name as William, rather than Philip, although Philip seems to be the correct name. Finally, the name of the first policeman on the scene is given as both PC Penfold and PC Pemblow in various accounts of the murder.

20

'IF YOU EVER LEAVE ME, YOU WILL GO A LIMB SHORT'

Southampton, 1896

In 1896, Brooklyn Road (now Belgrave Road) in Portswood, Southampton, was not a particularly salubrious area of the city. Nevertheless, eleven-year-old Sarah Matilda Philpott enjoyed making regular visits to the woman she knew as 'Mrs Burden' at her home there, often running errands for her.

Sarah was not aware that her friend's real name was Angelina Faithfull. Angelina had left her husband in 1893 and moved in with dock labourer Frederick Burden in late 1895. In the three months that they had lived together, Angelina and Frederick had enjoyed a rather stormy love-hate relationship, their frequent arguments usually fuelled by Angelina's love of drink.

On 19 February, Sarah called in to visit Angelina, finding her in the midst of another row with Frederick. Angelina had already spent time in the pub that day and seemed quite drunk, her tongue loosened by the effects of the alcohol that she had consumed. However, the argument soon petered out and Sarah stayed with Mrs Burden for a couple of hours that afternoon before going home.

She next called on the Burdens at lunchtime on the following day. Unusually, the front door of the house wouldn't open but, undeterred, Sarah went in through the back door. Finding no trace of her friend, Sarah began to walk from room to room, calling Mrs Burden's name. She found her lying on the bed in the front bedroom, her clothes and bedclothes soaked with blood.

Sarah ran from the house screaming, the sound of which brought out two near neighbours of the Burdens, who rushed to see what was upsetting the child so. After coaxing her story from the hysterical Sarah, Mrs Annie Nicholls and Charles Murray went into the Burden's house to check, finding Angelina lying on her side, clutching a razor in her right hand. Her head hung over the edge of the bed and her throat was cut so deeply that the blade had nicked her spine.

The police and a doctor were called. Dr Ives inspected the body and came to the conclusion that, although the razor Angelina that was holding could have made the wound in her throat, the cut was too deep for her to have made it herself, particularly as the blade of the razor was turned away from the body. Ives told the police that someone else had cut Angelina's throat and then placed the razor in her hand to make her death look like suicide – in other words, she had been brutally murdered.

With no sign of Frederick Burden, tracing and interviewing him was the top priority. On 22 February, the police went to his father's house in Middle Street, Southampton, where they found twenty-four-year-old Burden and immediately charged him with the wilful murder of his common-law wife. Frederick made a statement in which he maintained his innocence. He told Detective Inspector Boggeln that he had left Angelina after the row on the afternoon of 19 February and set out to walk towards Winchester. Burden insisted that he had known nothing about the murder until he read about it in a newspaper in Salisbury, at which he immediately turned back for Southampton in order to clear his name.

Frederick Burden was brought for trial before Mr Justice Day at the next Hampshire Assizes at Winchester. Mr C.T. Giles MP and Mr W.M. Barnes appeared for the prosecution, while Burden, who pleaded 'Not Guilty', was defended by Mr Bullen.

Mr Giles admitted in his opening address that there was no direct evidence to connect Burden with the murder of Angelina Faithfull but, if he were innocent, then it was a strange coincidence that he would choose to leave the home he shared with the dead woman at the exact time of her murder.

Young Sarah Philpott was called as the first witness and described her visits to 'Mrs Burden' on 19 and 20 February. Sarah was asked if she had ever seen other men at the house while Mr Burden was not there, a question that seemed to confuse her. Having first answered 'Not that I know of,' she quickly changed her reply to 'Yes, but not very often.' Several subsequent witnesses were to comment adversely about Angelina's 'immoral lifestyle', although none gave any more specific details.

Inspector Hurst, who had been one the first police officers on the scene, told the court that the victim had been found stiff and cold in her bed, covered with a sheet, a blanket and a quilt. Below the waist, she was fully dressed but was wearing only a vest on the top half of her body. Hurst related finding a blood-soaked towel beneath the bed, saying that it appeared to have been used to wipe up blood. There were also several spots of blood in other parts of the room.

According to Dr Ives, Angelina's death had occurred between seven o'clock in the evening and midnight on 19 August. Ives had been called to examine Frederick Burden on his arrest and had noted that Burden had half a dozen recent wounds on his throat, most of which were superficial, although two had penetrated quite deeply into his flesh. Burden explained that he had fallen into a barbed-wire fence but Ives believed that the wounds had been made by a sharp object and that the bloodstains found on Burden's clothes after his arrest were too extensive to have come from the injuries to his throat alone. The presence of spots of blood by the fireplace in the bedroom at Brooklyn Road seemed to indicate that someone other than the victim had been injured in the room, dripping blood as he or she walked about.

The prosecution then called Annie Nicholls, who had gone into the house after Sarah's hurried exit. Mrs Nicholls also hinted that Angelina lived an immoral life and told the court that there was a history of violence between the defendant and the victim. Angelina was found with bruises all over her body and, according to Mrs Nicholls, she visited Angelina and Burden about three weeks before the murder and found her struggling to breathe and in obvious pain. 'Have you been beating her?' she asked Burden, to which the reply was a terse denial.

'I shall have to leave him,' said Angelina.

London Road, Southampton. (Author's collection)

High Street, Southampton. (Author's collection)

'If you ever leave me, you will go a limb short,' threatened Fred.

Just days later, Angelina told Mrs Nicholls that Fred had tried to strangle her and that he was also giving her poison. Fred denied both of these allegations, going as far as to pour two glasses of beer from the jug that Angelina insisted had been poisoned and drinking them straight down, one after the other. Within minutes, he was violently sick out of the window, although the defence insisted that this was merely down to the rapid consumption of the beer rather than the presence of any poison. Frederick, Angelina and Mrs Nicholls then left the house together to walk to the pub and, when they left, Fred had walked off alone towards Swaythling, rather than returning to the house.

The prosecution then called woodman Stephen Paddick, who testified to seeing Frederick Burden near Romsey at about seven o'clock on the morning of 21 February. Burden asked Paddick if he was on the right road for Salisbury then conversationally asked him, 'Have you heard of a murder at Southampton?'

Mr Giles then summed up the case for the prosecution. Just eighteen days before Angelina's death, she had taken out a small insurance policy on her life. Giles pointed out a history of violence between the victim and the defendant and stated that Burden was known to have been with Angelina at seven o'clock on the night of the murder. On his arrest, his clothes were found to be bloodstained and there was too much blood on his garments to support his explanation of a fall onto some barbed wire. Not only that, but Dr Ives believed that the throat wounds were not consistent with injuries from barbed wire but were more likely to have been made with a sharp instrument

Burden was seen within 500 yards of Brooklyn Road early on Thursday morning at a time when he insisted that he was in Winchester and, the next day, he had asked Mr Paddick if he had heard any news of a murder in Southampton, which suggested that he already had personal knowledge of Angelina's death. At that time, Burden was on his way to Salisbury and he later told the police that he had first learned that she had died when he read about it in a newspaper there.

The defence insisted that the evidence connecting Burden with the murder was only circumstantial and that it was very weak.

Burden had been a respectable, hard-working man until he met Angelina Faithfull, a woman who, since leaving her husband, had been supporting herself by prostitution. Having persuaded Burden to live with her, Angelina had ensured that he was disowned by all of his family and friends. Even while living with Burden, Angelina had continued to encourage male visitors to the house and there was nothing to suggest that she hadn't been killed by one of these men. The house in which she lived was in a particularly rough area and was bordered by a public alleyway – anyone could have walked off the street into the house and killed her.

If Burden had committed the murder – and there was not a shred of evidence to say that he had – why would he have returned to Southampton rather than fleeing as far away as he could in the interval between the murder and the finding of the body? Why had he left a lamp burning in the bedroom, knowing that it would attract attention, rather than leaving the room in darkness? Mr Barnes insisted that Burden could have read a newspaper billboard before meeting Mr Paddick and learned of the murder in that way, before reading about it in more detail in Salisbury.

Burden's trial occurred two years before the Criminal Evidence Act of 1898, which established the right of a defendant to testify in his own defence and be cross-examined. Mr Barnes told the court that it was a shame that Burden was not allowed to testify and thus clear his name.

In his summary of the case for the jury, Mr Justice Day instructed them to put aside the fact that the victim appeared to be 'a loose woman' – even supposing it were true, that fact did not exonerate her murderer. The medical evidence had proved that this was a case of murder rather than suicide and the job of the jury was to decide whether or not they believed that she had died at Burden's hand. Day mentioned Burden's assertion that he had been in Winchester at nine o'clock on the morning of 20 February which was in direct contradiction to the testimony of a witness who had seen him near his home at the same time. It was up to the jury to determine which account they believed but, if they had any reasonable doubt, the defendant should be given the benefit of it and they should return a verdict of 'Not Guilty'.

Three hours later, the jury were still deliberating and when Day sent for them he was informed by the foreman that the jury was deadlocked and could not agree on a verdict. 'Would another hour help you?' asked the judge, to which the foreman replied that they were unlikely to agree, even if they debated all night.

This stalemate left Day with no option but to discharge the jury and order another trial. Rather than delaying matters until the next assizes, space was cleared in the calendar and a new trial opened two days later before a fresh jury.

Naturally, most of the evidence was the same as that presented at the first trial, although there were a few new revelations. It emerged that Angelina was often seen drunk and also that there had been an early edition of the *Southern Echo* newspaper published on the afternoon of 20 February and containing a brief account of the murder. Thus it was perfectly possible that Burden had seen a newspaper report before meeting Paddick and that, having read about the murder in more detail on reaching Salisbury, had immediately set off back to Southampton to clear his name. Why on earth, asked the counsel for the defence, would a guilty man have returned to the scene of the crime rather than putting as much distance between himself and the murder as he possibly could?

This time the jury took just thirty minutes of deliberation to return a verdict of 'Guilty', although they recommended mercy for Burden in view of the fact that he was only twenty-three and was of previous good character and that the victim's behaviour might be seen as having provoked her death. Asked by the judge if he had anything to say, Burden replied, 'All I can say is that I didn't do it.'

The jury's recommendation came to nothing as Burden was hanged at Winchester Prison on 27 July 1896 in a triple hanging. He shared the scaffold with two other murderers – Philip Matthews (*see* chapter 19) and Private Samuel Smith, who shot Corporal Robert Payne at Aldershot.

21

'POOR BABY IS SO ILL'

Rowney, 1898

On 14 June 1898, Henry Bailey of Portsea was walking along a road near Rowney church with his wife, Elizabeth. The couple were happily picking wild flowers, when Henry happened to glance down into a dry ditch, where he spotted a neatly wrapped brown paper parcel. Curiosity compelled him to unwrap it, although he probably rued the compulsion to his dying day, since the parcel contained a sack, in which was the naked and dead body of a baby girl. The infant, who about one year old, was folded double, her legs tied tightly around her neck with tape.

Bailey flagged down milkman George Wilson, who contacted the police on his behalf. Sergeant Adams was immediately despatched from Fareham police station to collect the macabre parcel, returning with Mr and Mrs Bailey, who willingly submitted to questioning.

Dr H.D. Brook of Fareham initially examined the baby on the day of the discovery of her body. He found the little girl's face and head to be grossly swollen. A piece of tape had been tied tightly around her neck and then looped around her ankles, drawing her feet up towards her head. Brook carried out a post-mortem examination the following morning and determined that the child weighed around 20lb, which was, if anything, slightly above the normal weight for a child of her age. Whoever the little girl was, she had obviously been well nourished and well cared for before her death, since she was a decidedly plump baby.

The doctor determined the cause of the baby's death to have been strangulation with the tape found around her neck. He noted that there were no marks around the child's ankles, a fact which suggested that she had already been dead when the tape was looped around them.

Meanwhile, rag-and-bone man John Robinson's wife, Alice, and daughter, Kate, were missing from their home in Waterman's Passage in Portsea. Robinson had rowed with his wife on the morning of 11 June, after he discovered that, not for the first time, she had spent the money he had given her to pay the rent on something else. When Robinson returned from work that evening and found Alice and Kate missing, he reported their disappearance to the police. Although his wife had always been a devoted mother to their daughter and had never before threatened to harm the child in any way, Robinson had a sudden, terrible premonition that she might kill little Kate.

Two days later, Robinson received a letter from his missing wife. Dated 12 June, the letter informed John that Alice was leaving Portsmouth for good and going to Walthamstow '... out of his way.' 'You need not seek for me as no doubt you don't care whether I live or die,' continued the letter.

Alice told her husband that she was taking 'baby' with her as – apart from her mother – Kate was all that Alice had left in the world. 'Poor baby is so ill,' wrote Alice. 'Pray God to save her. I am so miserable and unhappy but I hope you will have me back again when your anger has worn off.' The letter was signed 'yours truly, Alice Robinson,' but Alice had added a postscript after her signature. 'Think of baby if you cannot think kindly of me: and, oh, dear, do forgive me: I am truly sorry.'

Thus the police already had a report of a missing baby girl and summoned John Robinson to Fareham to inspect the body of the murdered child. John and his mother-in-law, Sarah Morgan, instantly identified the tiny corpse as that of Kate Robinson. However, there was still no sign of her mother and the police issued a description of Alice in the local newspapers in an effort to try and locate her:

> Age 22 years, height about 5ft 6in, stoutly built, short dark hair, recently cut. Tattoo A.M. on one arm. When last seen she was shabbily dressed in a dark, double-breasted jacket with large buttons, black bodice and skirt, black straw hat with crown cut out and crepe filled in and black boots with cloth tops, very much worn.

By then, Alice was in probably the last place that anyone would think to look for her. In 1864, the British Parliament passed the Contagious Diseases Act, which allowed policeman to arrest prostitutes in specific ports and army towns, including Portsmouth, and subject then to compulsory checks for venereal disease. Those women suffering from sexually transmitted diseases were placed in a locked hospital for up to nine months or until cured and, even though many of the women arrested were not prostitutes, they still were forced to go to the police station to undergo a humiliating medical examination.

Although the Act was repealed in 1886, Portsmouth Hospital apparently retained a 'lock ward' and it was here that Alice Robinson was admitted on 11 June 1898. Alice gave her name as Alice Ingledue and told the doctors that she was twenty-three years old and that she lived in Havant Street, Portsea.

Portsmouth Dockyard. (Author's collection)

The local newspapers were full of reports of the dead baby at Rowney and, on 18 June, having read the reports of the opening of the inquest into the child's death by county coroner Mr E. Goble, 'Miss Ingledue' approached the nurse in charge of the lock ward and confessed to her that she had strangled the baby. The nurse went to the house surgeon, Mr Charles Allen Robinson (no relation to Alice Robinson) and reported what her patient had told her. Charles Robinson immediately notified the police and Sergeant Adams went straight to the hospital.

He was in plain clothes and made sure to inform Alice that he was a police officer and to caution her before asking her to confirm her identity. 'I am a police constable and I believe your name is Alice Robinson,' Adams said. The woman agreed that she was Alice Robinson and stated that she had strangled her baby and left her at Rowney on 11 June. Taken to Fareham by train, she told Adams that she had rowed with her husband that morning about the rent money and that he had promised to murder her when he got home from work later that day. 'I am sure I was mad but, never mind, I should not have done it if my husband had not always been on to me and ill using me,' she stated, adding that, in fairness, she had to admit that her husband had never actually raised a hand to her, only threatened to.

By the time the inquest was resumed at Fareham Police Court, the police had managed to trace several witnesses who had seen Alice carrying a large, brown paper-wrapped parcel on 11 June. The first of these was seventeen-year-old Charles Jordan, who worked for a marine dealer in Portsmouth. Jordan told the inquest that Alice Robinson had visited the shop on 11 June to sell some metal to the proprietor. Offered the sum of 2s 9d for the metal, Alice was asked to call back for her money later in the day when the banks were open but Alice was insistent that she needed the money urgently to pay her rent, so was eventually given the cash. Jordan recalled that Alice had a parcel with her at the time, on top of which was a child's red dress. She put the parcel down while she was dealing with her transaction and, as she was about to leave the shop, Jordan called her and asked if the parcel were hers. She thanked him, telling him that the parcel contained old clothes that she had to drop off somewhere, before tucking the parcel under her arm and leaving the shop.

James Warn told the inquest that, on the morning of 11 June, he had called at the Robinson's house to collect their rent. Alice had admitted to spending it and her husband had been very angry. 'In future, I'll pay the rent myself. You shan't serve me again like this,' he told Alice, who defiantly answered, 'We'll see about that,' and left the room, carrying the baby. Warn admitted that John Robinson had used a few 'sharp expressions' but said that there had not seemed to be any real quarrel or hard swearing.

Alice was spotted leaving her house carrying a parcel later that morning by a neighbour, who offered her a cup of tea. Alice said she would have one on her way back. She was next seen drinking a glass of ginger beer in the churchyard at Rowney, where she engaged in a conversation with Mrs Sarah Moor and her daughter. Neither of the women noticed any parcel.

Dr Robinson told the inquest that Alice had insisted that she wanted to be discharged from hospital in order to give herself up to the police. Once in police custody, Alice made a statement insisting that her husband had threatened to murder her and saying, 'I thought I would not give him the chance.' She tied a piece of tape around her baby's neck then left the house for about ten minutes and, when she returned,

The Hard, Gosport.
(Author's collection)

Kate was dead. She placed the body in a sack then wrapped it in brown paper, which she had purchased that morning. Then, carrying the parcel, she took some metal from her husband's stock and sold it to the marine dealer. From there, she took a tram to The Hard and crossed to Gosport by the penny ferry. She visited an acquaintance at Rowney and was given a glass of ginger beer. Alice admitted to dropping the parcel containing her daughter in the ditch before leaving Rowney. 'I done it all myself,' she insisted. 'No one helped me and nobody else knows anything about it.'

Perhaps the most tragic witness at the inquest was John Robinson who, before the start of the proceedings, had fallen in an epileptic fit on catching a glimpse of his wife arriving from Winchester Prison. Although Alice Robinson seemed largely unaffected by the inquest, she was completely unable to face her husband and buried her face in her handkerchief as he entered the court.

It took the coroner's jury only twenty minutes of deliberation to find a verdict of 'wilful murder' against Alice Robinson and she was ordered to appear at the next Winchester Assizes on a coroner's warrant.

The trial opened in a packed court room before the Lord Chief Justice, Lord Russell and Alice Robinson immediately pleaded 'Guilty' to the wilful murder of her daughter, Kate. The judge, who was visibly moved, repeated the charge against her that she had deliberately and wilfully murdered her child, asking her if she was sure that she wished to plead guilty. Alice was so choked that, although her lips mouthed the word 'Yes', no sound came out.

The judge asked her if she had anything to say why sentence of death should not be passed on her and she tried to say 'No'. With that, in the light of her confession and guilty plea, the judge had no alternative but to pronounce the death sentence.

He expressed surprise that Alice had not pleaded 'Not Guilty', so that her case might have been properly heard before the court. However, although his function was not one of mercy, he would bring details of her family life and relationship with her husband at the time of the murder to the attention of the proper authorities. Not unexpectedly, soon afterwards, Alice Robinson was reprieved and her death sentence commuted to one of penal servitude for life.

22

'VENGEANCE IS MINE, SAYETH THE LORD. I WILL REPAY'

Grayshott, 1901

In the late 1800s and early 1900s, the village of Grayshott, in the North East of Hampshire, boasted some very famous residents, George Bernard Shaw and Arthur Conan-Doyle among them. Another resident, Flora Timms, who started work as a clerk at the village post office in 1989, was definitely not famous. However, after her marriage, Miss Timms became Mrs Flora Thompson, who was later to write several books, including the *Lark Rise to Candleford* trilogy, recently serialised on television by the BBC.

The post office where Miss Timms worked until early in 1901 was run by Walter Gillman Chapman who, prior to taking up his appointment as sub-postmaster in around 1892, had worked as a joiner and cabinet maker for his brother, Ernest, who was a partner in a local building firm. Walter maintained a small workshop at the rear of the post office, where he continued to work at his main trade, in tandem with his post office duties.

Walter married Emily, a woman seven years his junior, shortly after moving into the post office. The couple went on to produce five children in quick succession but the marriage was not a particularly happy one as Walter constantly suspected his wife of infidelity. His suspicions were totally unfounded but, no matter how strenuously Emily denied his constant accusations, he continued to obsess about her imagined immoral behaviour with other men.

In 1901, Ernest Chapman happened to call at the post office to find his brother ranting and raving at Emily, calling her all sorts of unspeakable names and accusing her of sleeping with men who, Walter maintained, had been hanging round the house all night. 'I have a pistol and I will blow your brains out,' he told his wife.

Ernest sprang to Emily's defence. He remonstrated with his brother, calling him delusional and reminding him that he had never found the slightest shred of evidence to justify his accusations against his wife and, even if he had, he still had no right to speak to her in that way. Ernest told his brother that it was not up to him to visit vengeance on his wife, then quoted a passage from the Bible: 'Vengeance is mine, sayeth the Lord, I will repay.' Walter considered his brother's words for a moment then turned to his wife again. 'That is the text that stopped you having a bullet through you,' he told her.

Above: *A view of Grayshott.*
(Author's collection)

Right: *The post office at*
Grayshott. (© N. Sly)

With Walter slightly calmer, Ernest suggested to him that the couple should separate, warning him, 'you had better separate than have these terrible rows. It will lead up to something bad.'

Shortly afterwards, the relationship between Walter and Emily deteriorated to such an extent that Emily called a cab, hastily bundled all the children into it and ran away to her brother-in-law's house. Her husband promptly took a holiday, staying at a temperance hotel in Bournemouth for two weeks. On his return, Chapman swore that he would not take his wife back, yet in May 1901, he did exactly that. A heavily pregnant Emily and her four other children returned to the post office and the couple reconciled. Miraculously, Walter's insane jealousy seemed to have abated and the constant rows ceased. Emily told people that this was the happiest time of her marriage.

However, on 29 July 1901, the apparent marital harmony came to an abrupt end. Emily Chapman was bathing her seven-week-old baby in the living room and sent her maid, fourteen-year-old Annie Harding, upstairs to fetch clean clothes for the infant. As Annie walked up the stairs, Walter Chapman walked down and, shortly afterwards Annie heard the children crying. She rushed downstairs to see what the matter was and found Mrs Chapman sitting in a chair, her husband standing behind her, with something clutched in his hand. Annie Harding couldn't tell what he was holding but she quickly registered that the couple were struggling and that there was blood on Emily's clothes. Without waiting to find out more, Annie quickly snatched up the baby, who was lying naked on the floor, and ran out into the street to safety.

Sarah Symmonds and Edith Smith, the two post office assistants, soon joined her, having heard screaming from within the house and decided to run for assistance without investigating its source. Moments later, Gilbert Winchester, Walter Chapman's apprentice, arrived. He had been in the workshop, when he had heard the children's screams. After speaking briefly to Annie, Gilbert ran back into the house. The front door was open and the children were still wailing in the living room. As he looked through the open door, Gilbert saw Walter Chapman holding a limp Emily in his left arm. Seeing that Emily's dress and her arms were bloodied, Gilbert quickly left the house again and intercepted Ernest Chapman, who he spotted riding his bicycle to work at the other end of the village.

Sending Gilbert Winchester to fetch a doctor, Ernest rushed into his brother's house where he found his sister-in-law lying on the floor. Ernest gently raised her to a sitting position, hearing her make a few faint groaning sounds before she died in his arms.

He was still cradling her body when the doctor arrived a few minutes later. Dr Arnold Lyndon briefly examined Emily Chapman before pronouncing her dead. The front of her clothing was saturated with blood and, as Ernest had loosened the neck of her dress, it was apparent that she had several puncture wounds on her chest. The full extent of her injuries was revealed only when Dr Lyndon later carried out a post-mortem examination.

Lyndon found the blade of a wood-carving tool protruding from Emily's back. The blade was missing its handle – later found in the living room at the Chapmans' home – and had been driven into the dead woman's back to a depth of four inches, with such force that the doctor had to resort to using pincers to remove it. The tool had been thrust twice into Emily's back, penetrating her spinal column, but in the doctor's opinion, these were not the fatal wounds. Emily had a further six puncture wounds over her left breast, two above her breastbone and four more over her right breast. Two of these wounds had damaged her heart and both would have been fatal. In addition, Emily had cuts to her hands, fingers and her right knee, three puncture wounds over her left elbow, two on her left forearm and one each on her upper arm and left thigh.

Police Constable Merritt, stationed at Grayshott, had been summoned to the post office and found Walter Chapman sitting on his bed, his head in his hands. When Merritt asked Chapman if he was aware that his wife was dead, Chapman replied, 'I know. I did it. Take me away.' The policeman took Chapman to the police house and sent for Sergeant Nunn from nearby Whitehill. Nunn arrived three hours later, during which time Chapman had told Merritt, 'I know I shall have to stand before my Maker and I want no mercy. My intention was to have blown my brains out and settled the lot. I am only sorry that I have left my little children behind me.'

Walter Chapman was conveyed to Alton by cab and charged with the wilful murder of his wife, appearing before magistrates at the Alton Petty Sessions where he was committed for trial at the Hampshire Assizes in November.

The trial opened with the Clerk of the Court formally charging Walter Chapman with the murder of his wife, to which Chapman responded, 'I am guilty of manslaughter, not of murder.' His defence counsel, Mr Charles W. Mathews, immediately asked the judge, Mr Justice Bruce, to direct a plea of 'Not Guilty' to be entered in the records.

Mr Giles then opened the case for the prosecution, telling the court that there were certain circumstances connected with the case that might perhaps relieve the jury of some anxiety in reaching their verdict. He then went on to state that enquiries had been made into the accused man's mental state, of which the court would hear more in due course. Mr Giles then briefly described the events of the 19 July, calling Annie Harding and Gilbert Winchester to give their accounts.

Next to take the stand was Ernest Chapman, who, having told the jury of his part in the aftermath of the killing of his sister-in-law, was questioned by Mr Mathews about his brother's mental state.

Chapman told the court that his brother had been 'very strange in his manner' for the past three or four years. He had suffered from delusions, the most prominent of which being the idea that his wife was unfaithful and that he had not fathered any of his children. Although Ernest stressed that these delusions were completely unfounded, he explained that, in his brother's mind, they were completely real. Walter Chapman was also paranoid, convinced that there was a conspiracy against him and that detectives shadowed his every move.

In May 1901, Walter had given his brother a sealed envelope, on which was written 'To be opened in the event of my death. W.G. Chapman'. Ernest had opened the envelope after Emily's death to find that it was a will. It included details of the alleged conspiracy against Walter, naming the people he thought were responsible. It continued 'Last, but not least, my late wife can answer this question. She holds their character in her hands.' (The term 'late wife' had been used to describe Emily two months before her death.) Describing Emily as 'a woman deceitful and deep as hell ...' Chapman wrote 'I was ignorant'. Such was the strength of Chapman's convictions that he had actually sent a telegram to the postmaster at Petersfield with the cryptic message 'Diabolical plot to ruin me'.

Dr Lyndon took the witness stand and detailed his post-mortem examination. He then revealed that Walter Chapman had consulted him privately some time before killing his wife and that, as a result of that consultation, he had come to believe that either Emily was a very wicked woman or, more likely, that Walter was suffering from delusions. Lyndon stated that he had had insufficient evidence at the time to certify Walter Chapman and, had he known then about the telegram to Petersfield or the will, he would have had no hesitation in doing so. It was Lyndon's opinion that, at the time of the murder, the prisoner was insane and was therefore not responsible for his actions. Lyndon was quite convinced that Chapman had not appreciated the enormity of his actions, even though he undoubtedly knew that he was murdering someone at the time – he knew he was doing wrong, but was absolutely powerless to stop himself.

Dr Worthington, the medical superintendent of the Hampshire County Lunatic Asylum and Mr T. Decimus Richards, the medical officer of Winchester Prison backed up Dr Lyndon's views, both stating that they believed Walter Chapman to be certifiably insane.

The judge summed up the case for the jury, saying that they would probably be of the opinion that the prisoner committed the act he was charged with – that of causing the death of his wife by stabbing her. If so, then the only question would be whether or not he was responsible in law at the time the act was committed. The jury conferred for a couple of minutes, then asked if there were any family history of insanity, to which the judge replied that this would not affect their judgement. They must decide on the medical evidence presented in court whether the accused was, at the time of the murder, insane and thus not responsible in law. As expected, the jury swiftly returned a verdict of 'Guilty, but insane.'

In all, the trial had lasted for less than ninety minutes from start to finish, when the judge ordered that Walter Gillman Chapman, aged forty-five, should be detained in Winchester Prison pending His Majesty's pleasure. Chapman briefly covered his face with his hands on hearing the sentence.

He was allowed to see his two brothers and his sisters before leaving court to start his sentence. It is believed that he died in 1921, without ever having been released from custody.

23

'YES, IT'S A FUNNY JOB'

Gosport, 1902

In 1902, Clarence Buildings in Gosport was described in the *Hampshire Chronicle* as being '... occupied by a low class of persons' and consequently, it wasn't uncommon to see drunks in the area. Normally, drunken behaviour was the prerogative of the men and it was a highly unusual sight to see a woman 'racing up and down the yard like a madwoman under the influence of drink.'

However, on the night of Wednesday, 9 April 1902, that was precisely the spectacle that was unfolding before a crowd of people, who watched as Sophia Jane Hepworth, aged thirty, cavorted around outside her home for some time before suffering a drunken fit, at which she rushed down the street and threw herself into the harbour.

She was eventually fished out and dragged home by her partner, William Churcher, who was apparently mortified at her shameful behaviour. The neighbours, who had earlier watched her drunken antics, now heard Churcher loudly remonstrating with Sophia about her disgraceful conduct. The argument reached a crescendo at about 12.45 p.m., when Sophia was heard screaming, 'Bill, don't murder me!' After that, things quietened down and nothing more was seen or heard until Churcher was spotted leaving the house on the following morning, locking the door behind him. He returned that evening, then was seen leaving again just before eight o'clock the next morning.

Of Sophia, there was no sign and eventually concerned neighbours contacted the police. Police Sergeant Hawkins from Gosport police station arrived at 16 Clarence Buildings at about half-past two in the afternoon of 11 April, finding the front door locked and the blinds drawn. Walking to the back of the house, he peered through the small kitchen window and saw bloodstains on the floor.

Joseph Cousins, a newspaper boy, had found part of a woman's skirt and a key on the shore near Clarence Buildings. He passed these on to Sergeant Hawkins, who immediately tried the key in the front door of the house. When the door opened, Hawkins walked inside and made his way through the house to the living room, where he found the lifeless body of a woman lying on the floor, partially covered by a skirt. When Hawkins pulled back the skirt, he saw that the woman's throat had apparently been cut.

Gosport, 1950s. (Author's collection)

Hawkins sent for a doctor and, while he was waiting for him to arrive, he began to search the room, which was in a state of disarray. A pair of men's hobnailed boots lay on the floor next to the woman's body, liberally splattered with fresh blood. A mat, some pieces of carpet and a towel were also soaked with blood, as were a pair of corduroy trousers and a waistcoat in an upstairs room. There were two broken vases in the living room, one on the mantelpiece and another on a chest of drawers.

When Dr Hunter arrived at the house, he could do little but pronounce the woman dead. He conducted a post-mortem examination on the body on the following day and found a six-inch cut to the throat, which had severed the major blood vessels and the windpipe and was deep enough to expose the spinal column. Two more cuts ran above and below this wound, a four-inch slash beneath the chin and a five-inch wound across the throat. There were four stab wounds on the back of the woman's right arm and a further two stab wounds, each an inch deep, on the right shoulder. The woman's hands were slashed numerous times, with eleven wounds on the left hand and twenty-four on the right. Dr Hunter classed these as defence wounds, incurred while the deceased was fighting desperately to stop her attacker from stabbing her.

The body of the woman was formally identified as Sophia Hepworth on 14 April by her husband, William Hepworth, a tailor who lived in South Street, Gosport. Sophia had left her husband shortly after their marriage and had moved in with Churcher, with whom she had been living as man and wife for almost sixteen years. According to William Hepworth, who had last seen his wife a week before her death, Churcher had frequently threatened her with violence and she had often sported a black eye or bruises.

Meanwhile, a search had been instigated for William Churcher, who was found at a pub in Alverstoke on the night of 11 April. When arrested by PC Loder, Churcher's response was 'Yes, it's a funny job.' Taken to the police station at Gosport, where he was charged with Sophia's murder on 10 April, Churcher immediately corrected the policeman saying, 'You're wrong; it was on the Wednesday night I done it. She went down to the water to drown herself and I saved her. You'll find my wet clothes on the bed. I plead guilty to it that night.'

Later, Churcher asked PC Hoare, 'Do you think I shall drop or not?' When Hoare said that he didn't know, Churcher told him that he had planned to either give himself up or to commit suicide and that, when he was apprehended, he was in the process of going round to say his last goodbyes.

Churcher made a statement about the events of 9 April, saying that, when he left the house that morning, he and Sophia were 'as happy together as we had been.' When he returned at eleven o'clock at night, Sophia was drunk. He had tried to persuade her to come inside, but she had had a fit of drunken hysterics and had lashed out at him, before running off down the street to the harbour. Churcher had followed her, finding her standing waist deep in the water. He had dived in after her and dragged her to dry land, taking her home and trying to persuade her to go to bed and sleep of her intoxication. However, Sophia refused and continued to argue with him, eventually seizing a lamp and trying to throw it at him.

Churcher managed to wrestle the lamp away from her, but was not quick enough to avoid the two vases, which she threw at him in quick succession. At that point, Churcher admitted to being in a 'great rage'. He had a clasp knife in his pocket at the time and, although he couldn't recall taking it out, as the couple continued their lengthy struggle, Sophia was stabbed.

The fight eventually ended when Sophia fell to the floor, after which Churcher made a perfunctory attempt to tidy up, replacing the two broken vases that Sophia had thrown at him. He had then spent two nights at the house before his neighbours had asked the police to investigate and Sophia's body had been discovered.

Churcher was committed for the wilful murder of Sophia Jane Hepworth. His trial opened at Winchester on 2 July 1902, before Mr Justice Bigham. Mr Evans Austin and Mr E.B. Charles acted for the prosecution while Mr Brodrick served as counsel for the defence. Churcher pleaded 'Not Guilty'.

The court heard testimony from the police officers, William Hepworth, Dr Hunter and also from several of the residents of Clarence Buildings. One, Mrs Alice Watts, told the court that she and another neighbour, Mary Ann Freeborn, had been drinking with Sophia Hepworth in the Isle of Wight Hoy public house, in Beach Road, Gosport on the night of her death.

Mr Justice Bigham.
(Author's collection)

According to Alice Watts, when they had returned to Clarence Buildings, Sophia had been '... not drunk, but very excited and under the influence of liquor.' She and Churcher had fought in the yard outside their home and Churcher had knocked her down a couple of times. Sophia was calling Churcher 'all the names under the sun', accusing him of having an affair with another neighbour's daughter, Sal Ward, and threatening to throw herself into the harbour. When she had carried out her threat, Churcher had rescued her and Mrs Watts and another neighbour had helped him take her home and tried to put her to bed. Sophia would not listen to reason and continued to try and attack Churcher, at which he told Mrs Watts that it would serve her right if he gave her 'a bang'.

Other neighbours testified to hearing a prolonged violent argument and screams of 'Don't, Bill!' and 'Don't murder me, Bill!' coming from 16 Clarence Buildings on 9 April, the fight continuing unabated until the early hours of the following morning.

Churcher himself was called to the witness stand and repeated the statement he had made at the police station. Now he added that, during their struggle, Sophia had picked up a worn table knife and tried to stab him. The two had grappled together for some time before she eventually let go of the knife and it fell to the floor. Churcher admitted that the clasp knife produced in court as the murder weapon was his, but continued to insist that he couldn't remember doing anything with it. He could not recollect whether it was open or shut while in his pocket, nor could he recall taking it out of his pocket and using it to stab Sophia.

The prosecution and defence gave their closing speeches. Mr Evans Austin began by saying that the evidence against Churcher was practically uncontradicted. He continued by telling the jury that Brodrick was going to try and convince them that Churcher committed the murder as a result of provocation by the victim. Sophia's attempt to use a knife on the accused had only now been mentioned for the first time and that knife had been dropped on the floor before Churcher took his clasp knife out of his pocket. There were no extenuating circumstances and Mr Evans Austin warned the jury that nothing less than a verdict of wilful murder would suffice.

Mr Brodrick countered by reminding the jury that there had been no denial of the crime, but that the question was whether the crime had been murder or manslaughter. Churcher and Sophia had parted on good terms on the morning of 9 April and, by the time they had next seen each other, Sophia was drunk. If Churcher had felt cold hatred towards Sophia, Brodrick asked, why would he have gone into the water to save her? And, having saved her at eleven o'clock, could he have been actuated by malice aforethought a mere one and a half hours later, when he cut her throat? Given the shock of finding that Sophia was dead, was it not possible that Churcher was speaking the truth when he said that he couldn't remember even touching his knife? In such awful circumstances, it was quite believable that his mind might now be a complete blank on the subject.

The crime was not deliberated or premeditated, argued Brodrick, but was committed 'under the greatest and grossest provocation.' The verdict should therefore be one of mercy and, should the jury find the accused guilty of manslaughter rather than murder, the crime was still a hideous one and would doubtless be visited with severe punishment.

It only remained for the judge to sum up the case for the jury. He told them that the question before them was whether or not the accused was guilty of intentional murder, which they must decide by considering what he had actually done, not what he had said in court. Mr Justice Bigham reminded the jury that Churcher had spent two nights in the house while his victim lay dead downstairs. The number of Sophia's wounds were indicative that she had fought for he life and the judge asked the jury if this was consistent with a man who simply dealt a blow in uncontrolled anger or a man guilty of deliberately 'doing the woman to death'. The testimony of the other residents of Clarence Buildings, many of whom had heard Sophia pleading with Churcher not to hurt her, did not tie in with his story of acting in self-defence.

The jury deliberated for thirty minutes before returning with a verdict of 'Guilty of wilful murder', although their decision came with a recommendation for mercy on the grounds of the great provocation received by the accused.

Promising to forward the recommendation to the appropriate authorities but adding that, for his part, he could see no reason at all why it should be made, Mr Justice Bigham pronounced the death sentence. Churcher appeared quite unmoved by his fate, asking only that he be allowed to see his friends and relations.

In the event, the jury's recommendation was not heeded and hangman William Billington executed thirty-five-year-old William Churcher at Winchester on 22 July 1902.

Note: In various contemporary accounts of the trial, defence counsel Mr Brodrick is also referred to as Mr Bentinck.

24

'THEY WILL MURDER SOME OF US UP THERE SOME DAY'

Aldershot, 1903

Thirty-year-old Esther Atkins was an 'unfortunate' – a polite euphemism used in the early twentieth century for a woman who earned her living as a prostitute. As the contemporary newspapers delicately reported, Esther was 'not unknown at Winchester Prison' and, in October 1903, had only recently been released after serving her latest sentence there. On leaving the prison to return to her life on the streets, Esther is said to have remarked, 'They will murder some of us up there some day.' Whether or not she had a premonition about her own demise, her words that day were to prove uncannily prophetic.

On 6 October, Esther was seen plying her trade around the public houses of Aldershot, an area noted for its profusion of army camps. By half-past ten that night, she was in the Crimea Inn, although her stay there was relatively brief as she was quickly ejected by the landlord for rowdy and quarrelsome behaviour, presumably fuelled by alcohol. A man who had been drinking in the pub at the time was seen to follow her outside, as were two soldiers.

As a working prostitute, Esther most probably viewed the prospect of three eager clients as a money-making opportunity that was too good to turn down. She certainly made no complaints as the three men hailed a cab and asked to be dropped off at the Wellington Monument.

The two soldiers, who wore the uniform of the Scots Fusiliers, climbed into the cab with Esther, while the civilian, Thomas Cowdrey, mounted the box next to the driver, Mr Carter. As Carter drove, Cowdrey chatted to him amicably, telling him that the woman had about £10 or £12 on her and that he and the soldiers intended to have it. Probably fearful for his own safety, Carter said nothing as his passengers alighted but simply watched Cowdrey and one of the soldiers walk away with Esther towards a wooded area known as The Coppice. The second soldier stayed behind to pay the fare, disputing the cost of the journey with Carter and arguing with him for a short while, before finally paying and following the other three into the woods. Carter promptly returned to Aldershot, callously leaving Esther Atkins to her fate.

At around 2 a.m. on 7 October, Cowdrey approached William Smith outside the Engineer's Stables, which were situated about a mile from The Coppice. Cowdrey told

Smith that he had heard a woman desperately screaming 'Murder!' and had gone to see if he could assist her. He had found her being attacked by two soldiers but, when he tried to intervene, the soldiers had turned on him, hitting him on the head and telling him to mind his own business, threatening to beat him if he interfered. By then, the woman was lying on the ground complaining that she was dying and, according to Cowdrey, when they heard her say this the two soldiers ran away.

Smith advised Cowdrey to go to the Military Police, which he did, only to be told that he needed to tell his story to the civilian police. To his credit, Cowdrey went straight to the police station and by 4.15 a.m., was escorting the police and Dr Jones to the place where he had witnessed the attack. There the police found the battered, almost naked body of Esther Atkins.

Although Cowdrey baulked at approaching the body, he was prepared to give a statement, in which he told the police that he had seen two Scots Fusiliers attacking the woman. The police immediately arranged for the entire regiment to be put on parade and Cowdrey walked up and down the assembled ranks of soldiers, closely scrutinising every face. However, he was unable to identify the woman's two attackers.

Yet two members of the regiment were not on the identity parade. Twenty-seven-year-old William Brown and twenty-one-year-old John Dunbar had both been confined to barracks for an unspecified misdemeanour on the night of 6/7 October. In defiance of their punishment, both men had sneaked out for a tour of the local public houses, returning at 12.15 a.m. on 7 October. At that time, Brown asked another soldier, Private John Robinson, if he might borrow a towel, saying that he had some blood on his hands. He and Dunbar then went to the wash house together, returning after a few minutes and going to bed. On his return, Brown had with him a pair of woman's boots, which, when questioned, he said that he had stolen.

The Wellington Monument, Aldershot. (Author's collection)

Robinson reported the unauthorised absence of the two soldiers to his superior officers and, on 8 October, a second identity parade was arranged, this time including Brown and Dunbar. Again, Thomas Cowdrey was summoned to inspect the lines of men and picked out William Brown as one of the soldiers who he had seen attacking Esther Atkins. Brown was arrested and, although Cowdrey failed to identify anyone as the other assailant, on the following day Dunbar was taken to the guard-room for questioning, in the presence of civilian police officer Superintendent Hawkins.

Dunbar was asked whether he had been out of the barracks with Brown on the night of 6 October and, after a short hesitation, he confessed that he had. When Dunbar also admitted to having visited the Crimea Inn and met Cowdrey and Esther Atkins there, he too was arrested.

Meanwhile, Cowdrey had been freely discussing the murder with all and sundry and had made numerous statements to the police, no two of which were ever the same. The police began to suspect that he knew rather more about the murder than he was telling them. Eventually, the clothes that he had been wearing when he first reported the attack were examined and, when they were found to be bloodstained, Cowdrey too was arrested and charged with Esther Atkins' wilful murder.

By the time deputy coroner Mr Foster concluded the inquest on 27 October all three of the accused had already appeared before magistrates and had been committed for trial at the next Winchester Assizes. Dr Jones, who had first examined the dead woman at the scene of the crime and then conducted a post-mortem examination, gave evidence that Esther's body had been covered with bruises and bore eight major wounds, which he believed had been inflicted with a soldier's belt. The deceased had fought fiercely for her life and Dr Jones thought that there had been more than one assailant and that Esther was restrained during the attack by at least one person holding her hands. Jones attributed the cause of Esther's death to shock, exacerbated by the prolonged struggle against her killers, saying that he estimated the time of death to have been at around 11 p.m. on the 6 October. The coroner's jury recorded a verdict of wilful murder against Thomas Cowdrey, William Brown and John Dunbar and the coroner was particularly scathing in his censure of cab driver Mr Carter, telling him that had he 'acted like a man' and reported his conversation with Cowdrey on the night of the murder to the police then the victim's life might have been spared.

The trial opened before Mr Justice Wills on 24 November and was to last for four days. Mr C. Mathews and Mr J.A. Simon prosecuted the case, while the two soldiers were defended by Mr H.P. St Gerrans and Mr Spranger. Initially, Thomas Cowdrey was undefended although, at the request of the judge, Mr Charles agreed to undertake his defence.

The prosecution maintained that the motive for Esther Atkins' murder was either lust or robbery and called her landlady, Mrs Wharran, who testified that whenever she had any money Esther would keep it tucked in her stays. However, Mrs Wharran also stated that Esther very rarely had any money and sometimes asked her for the loan of a few pennies.

In the run up to the trial, each of the three defendants insisted that he was innocent, each laying the blame for Esther's murder on the other two men. Thus most of the case against them hinged on eyewitness testimony.

All three defendants were identified as having been drinking in the Crimea Inn when Esther Atkins was thrown out and all were seen to follow her out of the public house. Mr Carter, the cab driver, positively identified Thomas Cowdrey as the man who sat next to him during Esther's last journey and told him of the men's plan to steal her money. The argument over the payment of the fare had enabled Carter to get a good look at one of the soldiers and he was certain that that man had been Private William Brown.

It emerged that a lone soldier had been spotted by the Military Foot Police, hiding behind some trees on the Farnborough Road at 11.30 p.m. on the night of the murder. The soldier bolted when he was challenged and asked for his pass but the military police later identified him as Brown.

Mr Justice Wills. (Author's collection)

Private John Robinson testified to the fact that Brown and Dunbar returned to the barracks at 12.15 a.m., saying that, at the time, Brown had with him a pair of women's boots. A pair of boots belonging to Esther Atkins was subsequently found torn to pieces in the refuse bins at the Mandora Barracks, where Brown and Dunbar were billeted. Robinson, who was later commended by the judge for the clarity of his evidence and his unshakeable adherence to his account of events, also stated that Brown had told him that he had blood on his hands and needed to wash it off.

Cowdrey had blood on his clothes, which was significant since he had flatly refused to go anywhere near Esther Atkins' body when he led the police to the scene of her murder. He had been seen watching Esther in the pub and had left immediately after she was thrown out, when he was identified as having accompanied her in the cab to the Wellington Monument. Cowdrey had then further incriminated himself by his conflicting statements to the police. His defence counsel, Mr Charles, made a valiant effort to justify Cowdrey's ever-changing accounts by calling witnesses to testify that he was 'simple' and 'weak witted'. These included a policeman, PC Knight, who had known the labourer and ex-soldier for many years. Having heard Knight's testimony, Mr Mathews for the prosecution immediately asked if the defence were intending to plead insanity for Cowdrey. Mr Charles assured him that he was merely trying to offer an explanation for the variations in Cowdrey's statements.

While the evidence against Brown and Cowdrey seemed relatively clear cut, the prosecution was forced to concede that the evidence against Dunbar was less so. At the identity parade of soldiers, Cowdrey had failed to pick him out as Brown's companion on the night of the murder and Carter had been unable to identify him as one of the two soldiers who accompanied the victim on the cab journey to the Wellington Monument.

In Dunbar's defence, Mr St Gerrans protested the admissibility of his client's guard-room confession that he had been with William Brown in the Crimea Inn on the night of the murder. Dunbar's statement, said St Gerrans, had been given while he was under military arrest, in the presence of a superior officer. If he had refused to answer the questions put to him in the guard-room, his refusal would have been seen as a breach of military discipline. Thus his self-incriminating admission fell under a legal ruling that, when a possible departure from the truth was occasioned by fear or compulsion, it was clearly inadmissible.

Major Woods, who was in charge of the military police at Aldershot, was called to justify his questioning of Dunbar. When Woods emphatically denied any compulsion, or having used threats or inducement to extract information from Dunbar, Mr Justice Wills ruled that the guard-room admission was admissible.

Even so, it failed to convince the jury, who eventually acquitted him due to lack of evidence, while finding both Thomas Cowdrey and William Brown 'Guilty' of the wilful murder of Esther Atkins. Both men were sentenced to death.

Dunbar's acquittal freed him to discuss the case and, shortly after his discharge from the court, he made a controversial statement to an Aldershot newspaper, which appeared to cast grave doubts on William Brown's guilt. Many of Dunbar's fellow soldiers remained unconvinced by both his acquittal and Brown's conviction and the entire regiment apparently felt a collective shame for the murder, closing ranks and largely confining themselves to barracks. It therefore came as a relief to all concerned when Brown confessed his guilt in the days prior to his execution, particularly for the jury, whose verdict had been much speculated in the light of Dunbar's post-trial statements.

On the morning of 18 December 1903, William Billington led both men to their deaths, assisted by his younger brother, John. As William Brown stood on the scaffold he reiterated, 'Before I leave this world, I wish to say that I helped to do it.' Thomas Cowdrey, a married man with five children, died protesting his innocence. 'Give me five minutes to tell the truth,' he begged, adding, 'God help my innocence. I'm going to heaven. Brown did it, he has said so.' His protests went unheeded.

As the local newspapers reported that the two men died instantly at the hands of executioner Billington, a short paragraph at the end of the lengthy description of the double execution informed the readers that Dunbar had been arrested by the military police for drunkenness and that, in view of his conduct in relation to that incident and 'other matters', an application had been made for his discharge from the army.

Note: In some sources, the assistant counsel for the prosecution is given as Mr Senior, not Mr Simon.

25

'A GOOD SON TO A BAD MOTHER'

Pollard's Moor, Copythorne, 1913

At half-past six on the evening of 22 June 1913, George Penny left his home at Pollard's Moor near Copythorne and went to his work as a barman at a local public house. George shared the cottage with his mother, Mary Matilda (known as Matilda) and his younger brother, Augustus, who was visiting at that time. When George returned almost five hours later, the cottage was in total darkness but he found nothing unusual in that. He quietly made his way through the dark cottage to his bed, passing through his mother's bedroom on his way and noticing nothing untoward.

The cottage may have been dark, but for a while, it was not completely quiet. As George settled down to try and sleep, he could hear pacing feet and what he later described as moans coming from his brother's room, as if someone were repeatedly saying, 'Oh, oh, oh.'

George got up to go to work at half-past five the next morning and, mindful of the strange noises he had heard the night before, he popped his head round the door of his brother's bedroom to check that he was all right. Although Augustus' bed had obviously been slept in, there was no sign of him, which struck George as being rather unusual. Concerned, he went to his mother's bedroom, where he found what the newspapers of the day described as '... a terrible spectacle'. Matilda Penny lay in her bed, her head completely shattered by a gunshot wound. Her bedclothes and the bedroom walls were heavily splashed with blood and brain matter.

George immediately ran to fetch the local policeman, Constable Joyce, who in turn sent for the police surgeon. On examining the body of Matilda Penny, the surgeon determined that she had been shot from behind at close range.

A search was promptly initiated for the missing Augustus Penny, involving a large number of police officers from the immediate area. An eleven-year-old boy, Evelyn Light, came forward and told the officers that he had seen Gus climbing out of a well and running towards the hedge that bounded a nearby field. Superintendent Wakeford and Constable Viney went to check and found him hiding under the hedge at the edge of a wood, about 400 yards away from the cottage. He was arrested and taken to Lyndhurst police station, where he was formally charged with the murder of his mother.

Yet, although the police had arrested a suspect in the murder of Mrs Penny, they had still to locate the murder weapon. Six police officers spent most of the day painstakingly searching the lanes and hedgerows in the area and their diligence was rewarded later that same afternoon when the gun was found lying in a ditch on the side of the main Romsey road. Described as a 'converted rifle', the gun still held a discharged cartridge.

Meanwhile, back at the police station, Augustus Penny was being questioned and was making a statement to the police. According to Augustus, his mother had been taunting him about George, as she often did and, in a fit of anger, he had lost control and shot her with a gun he had previously borrowed on the pretext of shooting pigeons.

Matilda Penny was fifty-seven years old and, although married, was separated from her husband. She was not a woman of sober habits and frequently drank to excess. When the marriage had ended, the two boys had each chosen to live with different parents. While George remained at Pollard's Moor with his mother, Gus went with his father to live in Portsmouth and subsequently joined the navy. However, after twelve years service he had left and, on hearing that his mother had recently come into some money, had decided that it was high time that he paid her a visit. Knowing his mother's fondness for drink, he took with him a bottle of whisky.

Of the two brothers, thirty-five-year-old George was obviously his mother's favourite son – after all, unlike Gus, he had not deserted her when her marriage ended. Just five months before her death, Matilda had written a letter in which she had given George undisputed tenancy of the seven acres of land adjoining their cottage for the rest of her life.

Augustus was brought before magistrates at Lyndhurst police station and committed for trial at the next Hampshire Assizes. The proceedings opened at Winchester on 8 November 1913 before Mr Justice Low. G.W. Ricketts and E. Duke prosecuted while Blake Odgers defended.

Augustus Penny continued to maintain that his mother had provoked him. He stated that he hadn't realised that the gun was loaded and had just produced it to frighten her. His defence counsel made much of the fact that Penny had been drinking heavily at the time of the shooting, suggesting that manslaughter might be a more

A judge and escort outside Winchester Assizes, 1909. (Author's collection)

appropriate charge than murder. He also quoted Superintendent Wakeford, who had stated that he believed that Augustus Penny was 'a good son to a bad mother'.

However, the prosecution were quick to point out that Matilda Penny had been shot from behind, while lying in her bed with her back to her murderer. It was difficult to reconcile the position of her body and the location of the wound with the idea that any provocation had been taking place at the time of the shooting. Rather than shooting at someone who was viciously taunting him, it seemed that Penny had deliberately fired his gun into a woman who, if not actually asleep at the time, was lying on her side in bed.

It took the jury just thirty minutes to find Augustus John Penny guilty of the wilful murder of his mother Mary Matilda Penny, although their verdict came with a recommendation of mercy for the accused. When Mr Justice Low asked the foreman of the jury what grounds they had found for their recommendation, he replied that it was on the grounds of the character of Mrs Penny and the probable provocation that Augustus had been subject to. Having assured the jury that their wish would be made known to the appropriate authorities, the judge passed the death sentence.

Immediately after the trial, a petition signed by more than 300 local people, who were presumably familiar with the circumstances of the Penny family, was sent to the Home Secretary along with a letter appealing for clemency. The Home Secretary responded quickly, sending a letter stating that the case was receiving his careful consideration. However, all hopes of a reprieve were quickly dashed by a second letter from the Home Secretary in which he wrote that, after considering all the circumstances of the case, he had failed to discover any grounds which would warrant advising His Majesty to interfere with the due course of the law.

Penny was described as an exemplary prisoner while awaiting his execution in the condemned cell at Winchester Prison. Shortly before his death, he wrote to the Prison Governor:

Sir: I wish that all officers should be thanked for the kindness that has been shown to me during my incarnation [incarceration] in this prison before and since my conviction, including yourself, warders, medical officer and chaplain. Believe me, &c AUGUSTUS JOHN PERRY [sic]

Mr John Ellis and his assistant Albert Lumb executed thirty-year-old Penny on 26 November 1913. He reportedly died instantly and was subsequently buried within the prison grounds.

26

'I WILL KILL OR BE KILLED'

Thruxton Down, near Andover, 1920

On the morning of 25 April 1920, farm labourer Mr Burridge was cycling to work along what is now the A303 when he spotted a man lying beneath a hedge at Thruxton Down, about five miles from Andover. Initially, Burridge believed the man to be either a tramp or a drunk but, when he approached for a closer look, he realised to his horror that the recumbent man was covered in blood and was unmistakeably dead.

Burridge pedalled off to summon a policeman and the dead man was soon identified as Sidney Edward Spicer, a taxi driver from Salisbury, who was married with one child. Spicer had been shot in the back of his head, just above his left ear and his body then dragged face down for a considerable distance from the roadway into a field. All of his pockets had been turned out and there was no sign of the car he had been driving.

A preliminary examination of Spicer's body suggested that he had been dead for several hours. Police enquiries established that the last time he was seen alive was at around nine o'clock on the previous evening, when he had driven two couples and a soldier from Salisbury to Bulford Camp. Spicer had been with his current employer, Mr E.S. Rogers, for a little over a week and should have had a considerable amount of money on him, estimated at about £20. Thruxton was about seven miles from Spicer's expected route from Bulford back to Salisbury and the police questioned what he was doing there, wondering if he had picked up another fare at Bulford.

The police issued a detailed description of Spicer's missing car:

Darraq 12 h.p. 1912 pattern; touring body painted French Grey, upholstered in black leather. Five-seater with Riley's wired wheels, two Ford headlamps, electric rear lamp and two Lucas black side lamps, hood and windshield. It has an Overland dynamo, fitted with ordinary bicycle chain, black leather universal joints, Bennett carburettor, Bosch magneto and a home-made switch board. Bates re-tread tyre on near hind wheel, Michelin square tread back offside wheel, Bates re-tread tyre near side front wheel and Michelin on front offside wheel. Bates re-tread spare wheel. The bed spring near offside has been recently repaired. Registration number AM2290.

The abandoned car was eventually located two days later in Sketty Lane, an isolated area of Swansea. It appeared to have been roughly driven. One of the front wheels was buckled, two of the tires had been slashed and there were some holes and dents in the bodywork that looked as though they might have been made by bullets. There was no blood inside the car, the interior of which contained just two clues – a petrol can and a packet of cheap cigarettes, which had fallen under one of the seats.

Although nobody had seen the car actually being abandoned, the Swansea police traced a witness who had seen the car being driven in the town centre by two soldiers. An immediate watch was placed on the railway station and on all roads leading out of the town, although privately the police believed that the two men had probably gone into hiding somewhere in the Gower countryside. A second witness, Mr George Scott, placed the car near Newport, Monmouthshire, on Sunday. It had been in collision with a cow and its two occupants were engaged in trying to repair the damage done to the vehicle. Scott told the police that the car had eventually driven off towards Newport.

By tracing the car's most likely route from Bulford to Swansea, the police found two garages where the vehicle had stopped on the day after the murder. At eight o'clock on the morning of Sunday 25 April, the car had called in at a garage in Cirencester for repairs, leaving after two hours. It had then stopped for petrol at Gloucester and arrived at Swansea on the Sunday evening, where the driver and passenger had spent the night at the Grosvenor Temperance Hotel.

Having spoken to witnesses, the police issued a description of two men they wished to interview in connection with Mr Spicer's murder. The first was of the car driver, who was aged between thirty-five and forty years, 5ft 8in or 5ft 9in tall, of medium build, dressed in khaki trousers and a 'British Warm' (a type of army greatcoat). The man's uniform had a gold crown, indicating that he had attained the rank of company sergeant-major. His passenger was aged between nineteen and twenty-one, about 5ft 6in tall, with a full, clean-shaven face. He wore glasses and was also dressed in khaki, with the letters RASC on his shoulder straps and cap badge.

With this information, the police went straight to the Royal Army Service Corps at Bulford Camp where, after holding an identification parade, they arrested Private Harry Fallows, who they believed to have been the passenger. Fallows made a statement naming the car driver as Private Francis Percy Toplis, always known as Percy.

Toplis was born in Chesterfield in 1896 and had been a criminal since he was just a boy. He was first convicted in 1908, when he was given six strokes of the birch for obtaining two suits of clothes by deception. After leaving school in 1909, he became a colliery blacksmith but was sacked after being found drinking in a pub when he should have been at work. He then embarked on a life of travelling around the country committing petty crimes, which culminated in a sentence of two years hard labour, following the attempted rape of a fifteen-year-old girl in Lincolnshire.

His more recent military history was sketchy, mainly because much of it was Percy's own invention, as were the multitude of different identities he masqueraded behind. On his release from prison in 1914, Toplis joined the Royal Army Medical Corps and was sent to Gallipoli, where he was wounded. He returned home suffering badly from the effects of dysentery and was given light work in a munitions factory in Gretna. However, as soon as he was deemed fit, he was posted abroad again, serving in Salonika and Egypt, where he developed malaria and had to be shipped home. After a period of service in India, he returned to Blackpool in England, where he deserted.

By 1919, Toplis had joined the RASC and absconded from Bulford Camp, taking with him a Sunbeam car valued at £1,000. Having sold the car for £400, he audaciously returned to Bulford and slept there for several nights. Although arrested, he escaped and was officially declared a deserter on 26 December 1919. He was then imprisoned for fraud and, on his release in 1920, although still officially classed as a deserter, he joined the RAF as a mechanic, deserting again, and joining the RASC once more. He was again posted to Bulford where he served in No. 2 Motor Depot, and was believed to be heavily involved in the black market sale of army petrol.

On the morning of the murder, he had shown his Webley revolver to a friend at Southampton, Private Holdrick, telling him that he intended to use it. After killing Spicer, Toplis had met Fallows and offered to pay his return fare if Fallows would go for a drive to Swansea with him.

Now that they knew the identity of their fugitive, the police were able to issue a more detailed description of the man who was about to become 'Britain's Most Wanted':

> Private Percy Toplis, number E.M.T 54262 M.T. RASC of Bulford Camp. Joined the RASC in August and was reported as a deserter in December. Aged thirty-four. Height 5'8" or 5'9". Medium build. Fair complexion, slight fair ginger moustache. Fair eyebrows and hair. Smart appearance. Has posed as an officer of the RAF and is believed to have deserted. Was in possession of a Mark VI Webley revolver, which he is likely to use if challenged. Believed to be dressed in a blue suit with a fawn soft felt hat and habitually uses a gold-rimmed monocle.

Meanwhile, an inquest was opened at Thruxton Farm by deputy coroner Captain Clarke into the death of Sidney Spicer. Dr Farr, the police surgeon at Andover, had conducted a post-mortem examination, which suggested that Spicer had been murdered. Farr had found a single, somewhat flattened bullet embedded in Spicer's brain and, from the trajectory of the shot, concluded that the wound could not have been self inflicted but appeared to have been caused by a gun fired by someone behind and slightly to the left of the driver.

Private Fallows told of his drive from Bulford to Swansea with Toplis, saying that Toplis appeared nervous throughout the journey, particularly when he spotted a police officer. Eventually, Toplis had given him £1 for his fare to return to Bulford, and the two men had parted, promising to keep in touch.

The inquest jury eventually returned a verdict of wilful murder against Percy Toplis.

On 21 May, Fallows appeared before magistrates charged with harbouring and maintaining Percy Toplis after the murder of Sidney Edward Spicer. However, when Toplis and Fallows met up at half-past eleven on the night of 24 November, Fallows knew nothing whatsoever about any murder and had remained ignorant until he had read about it in the newspapers. It was shown that, as soon as Fallows returned from his jaunt to Swansea, he had been brought before his commanding officer and had voluntarily made a statement, which had been passed to the police. The magistrates determined that there was no case for Fallows to answer and he was formally discharged.

Immediately after the discovery of the abandoned vehicle, the police had made a thorough search of the area, in which they were assisted by a large number of members of the local community. (It was pointed out that the description of the driver of the car matched that of the main suspect in another recent attack on a Bristol taxi driver at Thornbury.) On 7 May, a chauffeur was shot at through the windscreen of his car on the Abergavenny Road. Ten days later, police in Denton, Manchester, pulled up every motorist who passed through the area and examined their driving licences, although they refused to confirm that this was part of the hunt for the fugitive. In spite of the extensive search, no trace of the driver of Spicer's car was found and, as a result, the hunt for Toplis became nationwide.

In all, there were more than 100 reported sightings of Toplis from all over England, Scotland and Wales. On 2 June 1920, there was great excitement when it was erroneously reported that Toplis had been arrested in Skegness, Lincolnshire. However, less than a day later, the focus of the manhunt had switched to Banffshire in Scotland.

There, a farmer, John Grant, noticed smoke coming from the chimney of a supposedly unoccupied shooting lodge on the Moor of Lecht, close to the village of Tomintoul. The farmer notified the police and PC George Greig was sent to investigate. In the company of the farmer and a local gamekeeper, John Mackenzie, Greig went to the hut where they found a man sleeping. Greig asked him his name to which the man mumbled in an English accent 'John Williams' (a known alias used by Percy Toplis). Told that he would have to come to the police station, the man swiftly ducked behind an iron bedstead and opened fire with a revolver. Three shots were fired, two of which seriously injured the policeman and the farmer, before the man made good his escape. He was thought to have worked as a labourer in Tomintoul for several weeks and was said to have been a taciturn, uncommunicative man, who kept himself very much to himself.

Nothing more was seen of the man for four days until a PC Fulton came across a man in RAF uniform, who was lying on a grassy bank about ten miles from Penrith, reading the *Weekly News*. Something about the man aroused Fulton's suspicions and he asked him

The Lecht Road to Tomintoul. (Author's collection)

what he was doing. The unidentified airman told the officer that he was on duty warrant, going on to admit that he was technically an absentee, having taken a few days too much leave. However, he assured Fulton that he was making his way back to his barracks.

Fulton asked to see the contents of the man's kit bag and, to his surprise, the man tossed it on the ground and stepped back a few paces. 'You might be the likes of Toplis,' Fulton joked with him, at which the man smiled grimly and said, 'I am not that fellow.'

Now more or less certain that he had found Britain's most wanted man, Fulton left as quickly as he could and returned to his home to study the description that had been circulated by the Hampshire police. He then got on his bicycle and cycled as fast as he could to where he had last seen the man he now knew to be Percy Toplis.

Within a mile of the spot where he had first seen the man, Fulton came across a group of women who pointed him in the direction that he had taken. After some searching, Fulton found the man hidden in bushes at the side of the road near Thief's Side.

'Hello, old boy. Is this all the distance you have got yet?'

In a flash, the man was standing before Fulton pointing a revolver at him. 'You are a smart man,' he told Fulton. 'I am the man you are looking for, I am Toplis. I shot a farmer and a policeman in Banffshire. If there is any hanky-panky, you go. I will kill or be killed. Up with your hands.'

'I have no chance against a chap like you,' Fulton told him, as he stood with Toplis's gun pointed directly at his heart. Toplis seemed to consider his situation for a few moments and then ordered Fulton to throw down his handcuffs and his truncheon. When Fulton complied, Toplis told him to promise that he would not come after him and, when Fulton assured him that he wouldn't, Toplis turned abruptly and walked away.

Fulton ran back to his police house and changed into his motorcycling clothes before heading 'hell for leather' to Penrith police station. Together with Inspector Ritchie and Sergeant Bertram, Fulton went back to the area by car, followed by Mr Charles de Courcy Parry, the son of the Chief Constable of Cumberland and Westmorland on his motorcycle. As the small procession sped through the countryside, Fulton spotted a man in civilian dress walking along the road near Plumpton, carrying a brown paper parcel. Something about the man's military gait drew Fulton to take a second look, at which he immediately recognised the man as Percy Toplis.

The officers stopped the car and turned round, soon overtaking the man and concealing their vehicle around a bend in the road, intending to surprise him. However, as they got out of the police car to confront him, the man suddenly changed the parcel from one hand to another.

'Look out! He's getting his revolver,' shouted Fulton.

Ritchie and Bertram courageously rushed Toplis, who had managed to take out his gun and now fired off three shots in rapid succession, fortunately without hitting any of the officers. Toplis then steadied himself to take proper aim and, as he did so, two more shots rang out from the guns of Bertram and Ritchie. Although they were later to say that they fired only to wound Toplis, the fugitive immediately fell down dead, shot through the heart.

Between his first encounter with PC Fulton and his death, Toplis had shaved and changed his clothes. The police were later to find the bucket of water he had used to wash and shave, a few discarded garments and a diary, which showed his movements over the past few weeks in a series of abbreviations. These included a reference to the verdict of wilful murder returned on him by the coroner's jury in Hampshire which was annotated on 26 May with the words 'Verdict. Rotten.' The diary confirmed that he had been in Tomintoul and noted that he had pawned his 'poor old watch', the ticket for which was found on him when he was shot.

Toplis's identity was confirmed by his fingerprints and, at an inquest held into his death, the jury returned a verdict of 'justifiable homicide'. After his death, he was linked with several other crimes, including the attack on the taxi driver at Thornbury, near Bristol, where he allegedly led the gang who were ultimately convicted. He was also suspected of having murdered a woman, Miss Florence Nightingale Shore, on a south cost express train in January 1920. Detailing his previous crimes, the *Manchester Guardian* stated: 'The record reads like that of an all round degenerate, with whom murder itself was a matter of opportunity rather than calculation.'

27

'I WILL MAKE SURE HE IS FINISHED AND THEN FINISH MYSELF'

Southampton, 1931

The telephone call summoning the police to the house on Regent's Park Road, Southampton was logged at 3.15 a.m. on the morning of 28 August 1931. Just a few words, quietly spoken by a man with an American accent, were sufficient to prompt the police to rush to the location of the call as fast as possible. When the police reached the telephone kiosk from where the call had been made they found the telephone receiver and the door and windows of the phone box liberally coated with fresh blood. They were able to follow a trail of blood across the street and up the garden path of a house, where they found pyjama-clad Andrew Frederick Neely slumped on his doorstep, a broken razor clutched in his right hand.

Forty-two-year-old Neely was bleeding profusely from a large wound in his left forearm. In the doorway of the house stood his wife, Dorrie, dressed in her nightclothes and cradling a small child in her arms. As he waited for the ambulance to take him to hospital, Neely asked a policeman, 'Is my wife all right?'

Neely's wife was not physically injured, although she was certainly very shocked. 'I done it,' Neely continued. 'I love my wife. She is perfectly straight. You will see all in a note on the desk.'

When the police searched the house they found more than just a note on the desk. In the bathroom was the Neelys' lodger of twelve months, Wilfred Simmons Powley. Powley had two large wounds on his head, beneath both of which it was later found that his skull was fractured. Obviously close to death, Powley was also bleeding from a number of wounds in his throat and left forearm. A large, bloodstained lamp, fashioned in the form of a lighthouse and weighing more than 6lbs, lay nearby and the police theorised that it had been used to hit Powley over the head, before his throat and arm were slashed with a razor. Under Powley's bed lay the body of Neely's greyhound, its throat also slashed.

The note that Neely had spoken of was one of three found in his study. Written in Neely's handwriting and signed 'A.F. Neely', it was headed '3 a.m.' and read:

I am perfectly sane and have, I hope, just finished off the snake who was robbing me of my house and my wife. I was determined that she should not be dishonoured like the other women he has done and realizing that I cannot be here to protect her, I think this is the only means left. Also as things are there will be no hope for me. I am going out myself. I will make sure he is finished and then finish myself. God bless you Dorrie but you know. PS He is also a self-confessed murderer while he was in Africa.

Andrew Neely worked as an electrician on board the ship *Leviathan* and, as a result, spent long periods away at sea. He and his wife had been happily married until they had opened their home to a lodger in January 1931. Although Powley was a married man, it appeared that he had deliberately set out to seduce Dorrie Neely while her husband was away at sea.

Neely found himself being slowly edged out of his own home by his lodger. Powley and Mrs Neely went into business together, forming a partnership in a second-hand car dealership. While Andrew Neely was at sea, a 'For Sale' board appeared in the front garden of his house, at which Powley remarked to the next-door neighbour, Sidney Brown, 'I do not know what the old fool will think when he comes home and sees the notice board in the garden.' Powley bragged to other neighbours that he and Mrs Neely were planning to buy a big house and let rooms and, on one occasion, when Mr Brown asked Rowley when his landlord was coming home, Rowley airily replied, 'Perhaps he won't come at all as a letter has been sent to him.'

Neely actually returned from his tour of duty on 25 August. Initially the three occupants of the house on Regent's Road seemed to be on good terms, although neighbours noticed that Neely's hair had turned almost completely grey and that he seemed somehow deflated and had lost his characteristic briskness.

On the evening of 26 August, professional footballer William Haines, a long-term friend of Andrew Neely, called at the house. He too found the Neelys and their lodger to be on friendly terms, although when he took a short walk alone with Neely, the desperately unhappy man seized the opportunity to confide in his old friend. Telling Haines that a woman had told him that he had 'the sympathy of everyone in the street', Neely said that Powley had already wrecked three homes and was now trying to wreck his. What happened when Neely returned from his walk can only be imagined, although the eventual outcome was the death of the man who he saw as a threat to everything in life that he held dear.

Neely's wounds were successfully treated in hospital and he was charged with the wilful murder of Wilfred Simmons Powley and with attempting to commit suicide. He appeared before magistrates at Southampton Police Court and was committed for trial at the next Hampshire Assizes.

His trial opened at Winchester before Mr Justice Acton on 7 December 1931. Mr H. Du Parcq KC and Mr E.H.C. Wethered appeared for the Crown, while Mr T.J. O'Connor KC MP and Mr J. Scott Henderson defended.

The prosecution opened by stating that the defendant had previously 'enjoyed the highest possible character' and was known for his honesty, gentleness and mild manners and also his sobriety. He held a good job as an electrician and, according to his employers, his behaviour on board ship was 'everything that could be desired'.

The prosecution maintained that, 'rightly or wrongly', Neely believed that Powley was attempting to seduce his wife and had consequently attacked him with such violence as could only be expected to cause his death.

From the evidence heard in court, it quickly became apparent that the word 'wrongly' did not apply to Neely's beliefs at the time of the murder. In direct contrast to Neely, Powley's character seemed, as the judge was later to say in his summary, '... as bad as a man's record very well could be.' A married man from Walmer, near Deal in Kent, Powley had deserted his wife and children and gone to live with a woman named Peggy, who he habitually referred to as Mrs Powley. In 1929, while co-habiting with Peggy, he was declared bankrupt.

At the same time, Powley had also been courting a single girl who had absolutely no idea that he was either married or living with another woman at the time. Powley, it seemed, made a habit of sponging off women and Mrs Neely, whose husband was frequently away from home, had undoubtedly seemed to Powley like an ideal successor to the unfortunate Peggy.

Having moved into the house, bought entirely with Neely's hard-earned savings, Powley determinedly set about taking it from him. Neighbours testified in court that, while Neely was away, Powley and Dorrie Neely acted like man and wife, with Powley behaving more like the master of the house than the lodger. With no regard for Neely, he had put his house up for sale, boasting of his plans to buy a bigger property with the proceeds and live there with Mrs Neely and, in all probability, with Neely's children too. Until Powley arrived on the scene, Mr and Mrs Neely seemed happily married and contented. During the time that Powley lodged with them, Neely saw everything he had worked so hard for slowly disappearing before his eyes.

PC Thomas told the court that, after Powley's death, two letters from Dorrie Neely had been found in his wallet. One of the letters read:

Dearest sweetheart – I can only write a little because I am very busy. I can find time to tell you that I love you, though. I find it easier to write it than to say it. That is a habit I suppose. Love from your Dorrie.

The prosecution theorised that Neely had initially attacked Powley while he was in bed in his room and, as a final humiliation, Neely's much-loved greyhound had turned on his master and tried to defend Powley against him. When Powley staggered to the bathroom, Neely had followed him and slashed at him with the razor before slicing into his own wrist. Bleeding heavily, his one concern was that his wife should not be left to deal with the aftermath of his violent outburst so he had gone to the telephone box across the road to summon assistance before going back home to die. When the police arrived to find him lying on his own doorstep, Chief Inspector Chatfield told the court that Neely had shouted in distress to his wife inside the house, 'You are laughing at me.' Since Dorrie Neely was married to the defendant, she could not be called to testify in court.

The prosecution's final witness was Dr Grierson, the senior medical officer at Brixton Prison, where Neely had been confined since his release from hospital. Having examined Neely four times during his incarceration and having listened to the evidence presented in court, Grierson was of the opinion that, when he committed the murder, Neely was not sane.

The counsel for the defence took the floor, telling the court that he had been intending to call two medical witnesses but after Dr Grierson's testimony he did not feel it was necessary to do so.

In his sympathetic summary of the evidence for the jury, Mr Justice Acton reminded them that the victim had wormed his way into Neely's home and had then somehow succeeded in winning the affections of the defendant's wife, to whom Neely was devoted. In doing so, he had corrupted the mind of Mrs Neely, to all intents and purposes making himself the master of 'the little house in which previously a delightfully happy and contented domestic life had been lived.' He had indeed become the virtual master of the house, with the right to dispose of not only the mind, body and soul of Mrs Neely but also the very property that had been bought by her husband's savings. In consequence, '... under the accumulating influence of that infamous man', Neely had visibly aged. His hair had turned grey and he was unable to eat or sleep properly, until finally he reached the point where his tortured mind gave way and the shocking affair took place.

The jury didn't even feel the need to retire to consider their verdict and, after a brief consultation, pronounced the defendant 'Guilty but insane' on the charges of murder and of attempted suicide. Neely was ordered to be detained at the King's pleasure, while the ultimate fate of his faithless wife is not recorded.

28

'THERE JUST HAS TO BE
AN END TO IT'

Southampton, 1932

Catherine Harrington was a successful businesswoman, holding a position of some responsibility as the manageress of Arney's Laundry at Portswood Road, Southampton. Known to her friends as ambitious but level-headed, in 1916 she surprised everyone by falling head over heels in love with a man who was fourteen years her senior.

The object of Catherine's devotion was John Farrar-Hardwick, a sergeant-major in the Royal Army Service Corps, a flamboyant, brash, larger-than-life figure of a man who exuded self-confidence to the extent that many dismissed him as a show-off. Catherine's mother, Sarah, was one such person but, as she got to know her future son-in-law better, she recognised that beneath the bragging and posturing lurked a caring, sensitive man, who undoubtedly returned the love that her daughter felt for him.

John and Catherine married in September 1922 and set up home in the house adjoining the laundry that Catherine had previously shared with her mother. By now, John had left the army and, at Catherine's suggestion, came into business with her and began to work on expanding the laundry. A charming and personable man, John managed to attract many new accounts. His efforts led to a great increase in custom and for the next few years, the Farrar-Hardwicks enjoyed the rewards of their hard work and dedication.

However, in 1932, Catherine suffered a nervous breakdown, most probably due to the couple's intense workload. As a result of her illness, she became child-like and almost helpless, leaving John to keep the business afloat single-handed, as well as caring for his wife twenty-four hours a day. He made no complaint to anybody, continuing to be a devoted and caring husband but the strain soon began to tell on him. Catherine's mother helped with her daughter's daily care as much as she could but John seemed reluctant to delegate responsibility for Catherine's wellbeing to anyone, wanting to do everything for his wife himself.

To try and ease John's workload, Catherine's sister, Mrs Irene Lane, moved from her home in Leicestershire to help look after her. Even so, John continued to shoulder the burden of the majority of his wife's care, often going without sleep to do so.

By October 1932, it was obvious to everyone that John was fast reaching the end of his tether and, on 12 October, he finally confided in Mrs Louise Drage, a stewardess at the

Portswood and Highfield Unionist Club. 'I'll crack up if I don't talk to someone,' he told Mrs Drage, continuing to relate some of the day-to-day problems of caring for his wife to the sympathetic stewardess.

John told her that the pressure of running a business in tandem with caring for his wife was becoming intolerable. He tearfully related going out for a business meeting and returning home to find Catherine lying face down on the floor. Catherine had not recognised her husband and had fought him tooth and nail as he tried to carry her upstairs to her bed.

Mrs Drage suggested sending Catherine away to a convalescent home to give him some respite but John told her that his wife's doctors would not permit it. 'There just has to be an end to it,' John said sadly. 'I just can't continue.'

On 16 October, John decided to take his wife for a run out in the car to Winchester. They were gone for most of the morning and, when they returned home, Sarah and Irene noticed a change in the couple. Catherine seemed much brighter – almost cheerful – and John looked far less tired and strained than he had done in recent weeks. Having eaten a lunch prepared for them by Catherine's mother, John announced his intention of spending the afternoon at the laundry bringing the books up to date. Catherine had shown no interest whatsoever in the business since the onset of her illness but now she surprised everyone by asking to go with him.

Promising to be back in a couple of hours, John and Catherine set off to the laundry together. When they hadn't returned by five o'clock, Sarah and Irene began to worry that Catherine might be overdoing things. They went to the laundry to check that everything was all right but, when they got there, they found it locked and apparently deserted. Not having a key, they could do little but return home, where they tried to convince each other that John and Catherine had simply got involved in some business scheme or other and lost track of the time. By half-past six that evening, with no sign of John and Catherine's return, the two women were beginning to feel a rising sense of panic.

Sarah sent her daughter to the home of the laundry supervisor to borrow a key but, when Irene arrived, she found nobody at home. Sarah suggested that she go to the laundry engineer's home but Mr Spalding didn't possess a key to the building. By the time they managed to track down a spare key, darkness had fallen and Sarah and Irene were too afraid to enter the building alone.

They telephoned Phillip Summerbee, a friend of John and Catherine's, asking him to drive round and investigate the laundry with them. Although Summerbee obviously believed that John and Catherine had just gone off out somewhere, he agreed to humour the two frightened women and together they let themselves into the darkened laundry.

At first, there was no sign of the missing couple, until Summerbee walked into the airing room at the rear of the building. There on the floor lay the bodies of John and Catherine Farrar-Hardwick, both shot through the mouth. Death had not loosened John's grip on a Colt revolver, the butt of which was tied with a piece of string and Catherine was tightly clutching the end of the string.

The police were called and they soon found Catherine's handbag on top of a waste bin near her body. The bag contained three letters, all of which were in Catherine's handwriting. The first was a makeshift will, which read, 'Everything I have I leave to my dear mother to do with as she pleases.' The other two notes were to a creditor of the laundry business and to Catherine's doctor, Dr McDowell, thanking him for his kind treatment of her during her illness.

*Town Quay,
Southampton,
1950s.
(Author's
collection)*

The obvious explanation for the deaths of John and Catherine Farrar-Hardwick was that John had murdered his wife and then committed suicide. Yet everyone who knew him agreed that such an act was totally out of character and nobody could believe that John could have ever reached the point where he would consider harming Catherine.

An inquest was opened into the two deaths by coroner Arthur H. Emmanuel at which Emmanuel hinted that he had his own theory for what was behind the deaths of the Farrar-Hardwicks. However, he did not elaborate on his own privately held explanation, saying that it was for the inquest jury to determine what they believed had happened in the laundry.

The letters in Catherine's handbag indicated that she knew that she was about to die, suggesting the possibility of a pact between her and her husband. Although the coroner kept his own theories to himself, his line of questioning to the witnesses at the inquest seemed to hint that he thought that the couple may have been being blackmailed. Mr Emmanuel seemed to regard Phillip Summerbee with some suspicion, questioning him at length about his financial dealings with the couple. While Summerbee admitted to having received sums of money from John Farrar-Hardwick, all could be explained as payments for the hire of a car.

Had the Farrar-Hardwicks been blackmailed, it would have been reasonable to expect irregularities in the laundry's accounts. Yet, when the books were scrutinised by the laundry's general manager he was able to confirm that everything was as it should be.

In his summary for the jury, the coroner complained that nothing was fitting together. In particular he referred to the piece of string attached to the gun, asking what its purpose was and why Catherine had been holding so tightly to the end of it. It was suggested that the string was nothing more than a makeshift lanyard but that theory could not explain Catherine's death grip on it – had it been placed there by John to allow his wife a means of aborting her killing at the last moment by pulling on the string?

Eventually the jury returned the only possible verdict available to them – that Catherine Farrar-Hardwick had been murdered by her husband, John, who had then committed suicide while the balance of his mind was disturbed.

BIBLIOGRAPHY & REFERENCES

Books

Abbott, Geoffrey *William Calcraft: Executioner Extra-Ordinaire* (Eric Dolby; Barming, 2004)

Barton, John *Shocking Hampshire Murders* (Halsgrove; Tiverton, 1999)

Borrett, David J. *Andover's Mystery Murder: Who killed William Parsons in 1858?* (Andover History and Archaeology Society; Andover, 2005)

Bruce, Alison *Billington: Victorian Executioner* (The History Press; Stroud, 2009)

Browne, Douglas G. and Tullett, E.V. *Bernard Spilsbury: His Life and Cases* (George G. Harrap & Co. Ltd, 1951)

Casswell QC, J.D. *A Lance for Liberty* (George G. Harrap & Co. Ltd; London, 1961)

Eddleston, John J. *The Encyclopaedia of Executions* (John Blake; London, 2004)

Evans, Stewart P. *Executioner: The Chronicles of a Victorian Hangman* (Sutton Publishing; Stroud, 2006)

Fielding, Steve *The Hangman's Record Volume One 1868–1899* (Chancery House Press; Beckenham, Kent, 1994)

Fox, Ian *Hampshire Tales of Murder and Mystery* (Countryside Books; Newbury, 2001)

Guttridge, Roger *Hampshire Murders* (Southampton; Ensign Publications, 1990)

Newspapers

Hampshire Chronicle and General Advertiser for the South and West of England
Hampshire Telegraph and Sussex Chronicle
Illustrated Police News
Manchester Guardian
Southampton Courier
Southern Daily Echo
The Times

Certain websites have also been consulted in the compilation of this book, but since they have a habit of disappearing, to avoid frustration, they have not been cited.

INDEX

Abbot, PC George 35
Acton, Mr Justice 146-8
Adams, Private Benjamin 63-4
Adams, Charles Ashby 73
Adams, Sergeant 116-18
Aldershot 44-5, 48-50, 62-6, 67-70, 115, 130-5
Aldridge, Robert 11
Allan, James 27
Alresford 20-3, 51-5
Alton 101-2, 123
Alverstoke 126
Anderson, Duncan 49
Andover 35-43, 139-41
Atkins, Esther 130-5
Ayles, PC Stephen 34
Aymore, PC 11-13

Bailey, Charles 29-34
Bailey, Elizabeth 116
Bailey, Henry 116
Banks, Elizabeth 39
Banks, Emma 38-43
Banks, Thomas 38-43
Banks, Thomas Alexander 41
Barber, William 104
Barnes, Mr W.M.108, 112-14
Barnett, Harriet 34
Bear Hotel, The 81
Beauchamp, Captain Fitzmaurice 64
Beauclerk, Lord George 56
Bennett, Emily 40
Bentham, Mr (1860) 46
Bentham, Mr (1865) 58

Bere, Mr 55
Berry, James 70, 91
Bertram, Sergeant 143-4
Bigham, Mr Justice 127-9
Billington, James 103
Billington, William 129, 135
Binsted 100-3
Black, Mr 88-90
Blackbrook 11
Blackman, Dr Josiah George 88
Blatherwick, Thomas 11
Bleach, Mr 95
Blundell, Mrs 89-90
Boggeln, Detective Inspector 112
Bolland, Mr Baron 18-19
Botley 106
Bournemouth 122
Bovill Smith, Mr 81
Boyd, Captain 80-1
Bramdean 20-3
Bramsdon, Mr T.A. 74, 88, 95, 107
Brett, Corporal William 62-6
Brewer, William 100-3
Bridge Inn/Tavern, The 31-4
Brighton 21, 78-83
Brixton Prison 147
Broadmoor Criminal Lunatic Asylum 57
Brodrick, Mr 127-9
Brook, Dr H.D. 116
Broomfield, Ann 54-7
Broomfield, George 51-7
Brown, Mr (1860) 44
Brown, Mr (1864) 54-6
Brown, Ruth 38

Brown, Sidney 146
Brown, William 16-9
Brown, Private William 131-5
Bruce, Mr Justice 123
Buck, William 19
Bucknill QC, Mr 97-8
Bullen, Mr 102
Bunce, Private Robert 63-4
Burden, Frederick 110, 111-15
Burridge, Mr 139
Burrows, Mrs 51
Butcher, George 38

Calcraft, William 50, 61, 66
Campbell, Corporal 48
Carter, Private John 64
Carter, Mary 23
Carter, Mr 130-4
Cave, Mr Justice 88-90
Chambers, James 40
Chapman, Emily 120-4
Chapman, Ernest 120-4
Chapman, Walter Gillman 120-4
Chappell, George 100
Charles, Mr 60, 132-4
Charles, Mr E.B. 127
Chatfield, Chief Inspector 147
Checkers Inn, The 22
Chequers Inn, The 38-40
Chichester 78
Churcher, William 125-9
Cirencester 140
Clark, Charles (Havant) 80
Clark, Charles (Newtown) 68-70
Clarke, Captain 141
Clarke, George 67-70
Clarke, James 67-8
Clarke, John 44-6
Clarke, Lily 68-9
Clarke, Mrs (1860) 44-6
Clarke, Mrs (1888) 67-70
Clarke, Sarah 45-6
Clarke, Thomas 77-8
Clements, Charles 58-60
Clements, Maria 58-61
Cockburn, Mr Serjeant 27-8

Colborne (Wing) Caroline 51-7
Colborne, Frederick 51-4
Cole, Mr H.T. 50, 55
Coleridge QC, Mr 18, 55-6
Collier, Sir R.P. 64
Collins, Harriet 101
Compton, Mr 55
Cook, Fanny 71
Cooke, Mr 21
Cooke, Mr Temple 68, 81, 88-90, 108-9
Cooke, Mr W.M. 32, 46
Copnor 104-10
Cormack, Henry 50
Cormick, Andrew 49-50
Cosser, Chief Constable 92
Cousins, Joseph 125
Cowdrey, Thomas 130-4
Cricketer's Arms, The 101
Crimea Inn, The 130-4
Cross, Corporal James 62-4
Crosswell, Mr 22

Dacres, Admiral 9
Dampier, Mr 21
Davis, Mr 59-60
Day, Henry 37
Day, Mr Justice 97-8, 108-9, 112-15
Deadman, John 20-3
Decimus Richards, Mr T. 124
De Courcy Parry, Charles 143
Delap family 55-6
Denton, Manchester 142
Dickson, Sergeant John 48-50
Digby, Captain 8-10
Dixon, Private William 62-6
D'Onston Stephenson, Robert / D'Onston Roslyn 83
Dorey, PC Stephen 88
Dorey, PC Thomas 88
Downton, Edmund 92
Downton, Emma 92-9
Downton, Harriet (jnr) 92
Downton, Harriet (snr) 92-8
Downton, Willie 92
Drage, Louise 149-50

Dream 26
Duke, Mr E. 137
Dunbar, Private John 131-5
Du Parcq QC, Mr H. 146
Dyott, Charles 34

Earle, Mr Justice 27
Easton 75
Edwards, Revd G. 75
Elliot, Mr Jabez Henry 37
Ellis, John 138
Elson 13
Emmanuel, Arthur H. 151
Emsworth 77-82
Endymion 9
Evans Austin, Mr 127-9
Eyres, John 32-4

Fagan, Mr J. 7-10
Faithfull (Burden), Angelina 111-15
Fallows, Pte Harry 140-1
Fareham 11-14, 107, 116-18
Farnden, Mrs 80-2
Farnden, William 81-4
Farr, Dr 141
Farrar-Hardwick, (Harrington)
  Catherine 149-51
Farrar-Hardwick, John 149-51
Farrell, Albert 80
Feltham, George 80
Field, Mr Justice 68-70
Fiske, Thomas 25
Floyd, Mr 34
Folkard, Mr 97
Footer, Harry 37
Foster, Mr 132
Fratton 92-4, 107-8
Freeborn, Mary Ann 127
Fry, Sergeant 71
Fulton, PC 142-4

Gardiner, George 18-19
Garrington, William Hawkings 16-18,
  59-60
Gaselee, Mr Justice 14
Gethin, Richard 14

Giles MP, Mr C.T. 112-14, 123
Gloucester 140
Goble, Mr E. 79, 118
Goff, Detective 107
Golden Lion Inn, The 12
Gosport 8, 14, 24-8, 44-7, 107, 119, 125-9
Gough, PC 67-9
Gould, Mr 58
Grant, John 142
Grantham, Sir William 102-3
Grayshott 120-4
Greenwood, Mr 21
Gregg, John 64
Greig, PC George 142
Grierson, Dr 147
Grosvenor Temperance Hotel, The 140
Gunner, Mr 60, 71
Guyatt, Frederick 42-3
Guyatt, Martha 40-3

Haines, William 146
Hall, John 20-3
Hampshire County Lunatic Asylum 124
Harding, Annie 122-3
Harmsworth, William 11-14
Harrington, Sarah 149-50
Harris, Mrs (1864) 53
Harris, Mrs (1865) 58
Harris, PC Henry 11-13
Haslar Naval Hospital 8, 27
Havant 76-84
Hawkey, Henry Charles Morehead 24-8
Hawkins, Inspector 101
Hawkins, Mary 38
Hawkins, Mrs 75
Hawkins, Sergeant 125-6
Hawkins, Superintendent 132
Hayes, Henry 37
Hayley, Mr W.H. 63
Hayward, Sergeant 88
Heddington, Edward 67-9
Henshall, Private 62-5
Hepworth, Sophia Jane 125-9
Hepworth, William 126-7
Heroes of Lucknow Inn 67
Hickley, George 87-8

Hickley, William Harding 87-8
HMS *Asia* 61
HMS *Diadem* 58, 61
HMS *Resistance* 7-9
Hoare, PC 127
Hobbs, Mr 94-5
Holdrick, Private 141
Howard, Franklin 16
Howard, Superintendent William 48-9
Hughes, Private John 59-61
Hunter, Dr 126-7
Hurst, Inspector 112
Husband, Fanny 82
Husband, George 80-3
Husband, Robert (jnr) 76-84
Husband, Robert (snr) 76-82
Hutchins, David 45-6
Hynes, Michael 44-7

Isle of Wight 84
Isle of Wight Hoy, The 127
Ives, Dr 111-14

Jack the Ripper 78-83
Jackson, Private Thomas 48-50
Jee, Joseph 48-50
Jenkins, John 26
Jones, Dr 131-2
Jones, Eliza 71-5
Jones, Thomas 71-5
Jordan, Charles 118
Joyce, PC 136

Kay, William 101-2
Keating, Mr Justice 46-7, 55-7, 60-1
Kemish, John 32-4
Kile, Mr 22
Kingston 75, 93-5
Kinsholt, Superintendent 79
Knapton, Sergeant 79-83
Knight, Cyrus 100-3
Knight, Frances 100-3
Knight, PC 134

Ladbrooke, Revd J. 91
Lamb Inn, The (Fareham) 107

Lamb Inn, The (Romsey) 29, 34
Lancaster, William 88
Lane, Irene 149-50
Langridge, Helena Elizabeth Jane 94
Langstaff, Dr William 37
Lawler, Detective Inspector 80-1
Lawes, James 23
Leach, Emma 32-4
Le Blanc, Mr Justice 8-9
Lentall, Mr 35-40
Leviathan 146
Ley, Ellen 40
Light, Evelyn 136
Light, Jim Sampson 100-1
Liston, Robert 26
Liverpool 62
Loder, PC 126
Longcroft, Mr C.H. 12, 20
Longhirst, Mr 64
Loscombe, Henry 40
Loveridge, Joseph 95
Low, Mr Justice 137-8
Luck, Sergeant 107
Lumb, Albert 138
Lush, Rowland George 42-3
Lutwidge, Lieutenant Thomas Henry 7-10
Lyndhurst 136-7
Lyndon, Dr Arnold 122-4

Mackenzie, John 142
Maloney, Charlotte 106-9
Mandora Barracks 134
Marsh, George 64
Marsh, William 25-6
Marshall, Private William 48-9
Mathews, Charles 81-2, 97-8, 123,
    132-4
Matthews, Elizabeth 105
Matthews, Elsie Gertrude 104-10
Matthews, Maria 106-10
Matthews, Mr 30-2
Matthews, Philip 104-10
Maybrick, Florence 84
Maybrick, James 84
Maybrick, Michael 84
Maybury, Dr Lysander 97-8, 104-9

McDowell, Dr 150
McGee, Mr H.W. 108
McGregor, Dr James 88, 104
Merritt, PC 123
Mesh, Thomas 37
Millbank Prison 57
Miller, Mr 75
Miller, Susan 73
Minstead 29-34
Money, Detective Sergeant 94
Moor of Lecht 142
Moor, Sarah 118
Morgan, Sarah 117
Morgan, William 18-19
Morley, Frederick 74
Mott, William 54
Munro, Private 49-50
Murray, Charles 111

Naval and Military Arms, The 73-5
Neale, Mr 7-9
Neely, Andrew Frederick 145-8
Neely, Dorrie 145-8
Newbury, Mr 73
Newport 140
Nicholls, Annie 111-13
Northover, Henry Edward 35-7
Nunn, Sergeant 123

O'Connor KC MP, Mr T.J. 146
Odgers, Blake 102, 137
O'Neil, Private 60
Onslow MP, Mr 51-6

Paddick, Stephen 114-15
Pain, Mr T. 49-50
Parker, Private 59-60
Parsons, Mrs 37-43
Parsons, William 35-43
Pearce, John 34
Pearse, George 38
Penfold, PC 104, 110
Penny, Augustus 136-8
Penny, George 136-7
Penny, Mary Matilda 136-8
Penrith 142-3

Petersfield 21-2, 123-4
Petts, Mrs 22
Philpott, Sarah Matilda 111-12
Piggott, Dr and Mrs 104-10
Pilkington, Mr 18
Platt, John 76-84
Platt, Mr Baron 28
Plumpton 143
Pocock, Sergeant-Major John 49-50
Poland, Mr 38-41, 64
Poole, Detective Sergeant William 59
Porter, Inspector William 71
Portsea 58-61, 75, 116-17
Portsmouth 15-19, 24-6, 58-61, 68,
    71-5, 77-83, 85-91, 92, 95, 104-7,
    117-18, 137
Potter, Mr J.P. 26
Poulden, Mr 21, 41, 46, 60
Powell, John (Langley Pearce) 15-18
Powell, Mr 51
'Powley', Peggy 147
Powley, Wilfred Simmons 145-8
Prideaux, Mr 32
Prince Albert Inn, The 67
Profitt, Sergeant 49-50
Prouce, Heziah 16-18
Purcell, John 17
Pym, Lieutenant Edward 25-7

Quebec Hotel, The 26
Queen's Head, The 58-60
Quinton Bond, Dr S. 79-82

Railway Tavern, The 40-1
Rawlinson, Mr / Gunner 71-3
Reeves, Sergeant John 37
Ricketts, Mr G.W. 137
Ritchie, Inspector 143-4
Robertson, Dr John Robert Stephenson
    97
Robinson, Alice 116-19
Robinson, Charles Allen 118
Robinson, John 116-19
Robinson, Private John 131-4
Robinson, Kate 116-19
Rogers, Ellen 73

Rogers, Mr E.S. 139
Rogers, Mary 71-4
Romsey 29-34, 114, 137
Ropley 22
Rose, William 34
Rowles, Lieutenant Byron 25-6
Rowney 116-19
Royal South Hants Infirmary 54
Rubie, Mr 81, 88
Rummer, The 44
Russell, Lord 119
Russell, Mr C. 50

St Gerrans, Mr H.P. 132-4
Salisbury 112-5, 139
Sampson, George 26
Saunders, Mr C. 21, 32
Schoolbred, Dr 69
Scorey, Mr 20
Scott, Mr George 140
Scott Henderson, Mr J. 146
Searle, Percy Knight 76-84
Senior, Mr 135
Seton, Captain James Alexander 24-8
Sewell, Mr 32
Shackell, Mr 20-1
Shein, Ann 44-7
Shein, David 45-6
Sheppard, Moses 11-14
Shirley 51-7
Shirley, Henry 76-81
Shirley Hotel, The 51-4
Shore, Florence Nightingale 144
Short, Dr 55
Simms, Mary Ann 32-4
Simon, Mr J.A. 132, 135
Simpson, Edward 95
Skegness 142
Smith, Edith 122
Smith, Henry 40
Smith, John 80
Smith, Mr 103
Smith, Mr Justice Montague 64-5
Smith, Pte Samuel 110, 115
Smith, William 130-1

Soffe, George 29
Soffe, John 29-34
Southampton 22, 51-5, 111-15, 141, 145-8, 149-51
South Camp 62
Southsea 24, 92-9
Spalding, Mr 150
Spearing, James 34
Speyshott, Mr 13
Spicer, Sidney Edward 139-41
Spranger, Mr 132
Stansmore, Mary Ann 24-5
Stedman, Mr 107
Steele, Alfred 78, 83
Stephen, Mr Justice 81-3
Stevens, Thomas 80
Stevenson, Mr 8-9
Stockley, John Cowlin 40
Straight, Mr 64
Strangeways Prison 42
Strickland, John 18
Summerbee, Phillip 150-1
Sun, The 11
Swansea 140-1
Swaythling 113
Symmonds, Sarah 122

Talfourd, Mr Justice 32
Tatford, Henry 11-13
Tatford, John 11-13
Taylor, Detective 94, 109
Teignmouth 104-7
Temple-Cooke, Mr 68, 81, 88-90, 108-9
Thomas, PC 147
Thornbury 142-4
Three Tuns, The 13
Thruxton Down 139-44
Tidy, Professor Charles M. 81-2
Tilbury's Royal Hotel 49
Titchfield 11
Todd, Mr J.H. 54
Tomintoul 142-4
Toplis, Private Francis Percy 140-4
Turner, Mr 22
Tweed, Dr 56-7

Urry, Elizabeth (snr) 93-6
Urry (Whiting), Elizabeth Ada 93-9

Vaughan, Annie 67-70
Vine, The 22
Viney, PC 136

Wakeford, Superintendent 136-7
Walmer 147
Ward, Sal 128
Warn, James 118
Warren, Henry 9
Waters, Dolly 93-5
Waters, Mr and Mrs 93-4
Watson, Mr Baron 41
Watts, Alice 127-8
Watts, Arthur 85-8
Watts, Edward Henry Fawcett 85-91
Watts, (Hickley) Esther Emily 85-91
Webb, Francis James 38-40
Webb, William 32-4
Wedge, Superintendent Charles 35-7
Weeks, Thomas 38
Westcott, Joseph 106-7
Weston, Dr Philip King 53-4
Wethered, Mr E.H.C. 146
Wharran, Mrs 132
Wharton, Mr 45-6
Wheeler, Henry 80
Whelan, Kate 72

Whitbread, Ethel 80
White, Mr H. 101-2
White Hart, The 53
Whitechapel 78-84
Whitehill 123
Whittaker, Mary 74
Willes, Mr 69
Williams, Mr Justice 21
Williams, Smith 17-19
Willis, Charley 17
Wills, Mr Justice 132-4
Wilson, George 116
Wiltshire, Eliza 38
Wiltshire, Mr 29
Winchester 8, 14, 18-19, 21-3, 27, 32,
    41, 45-7, 50, 55, 61, 63-6, 69-70, 81,
    88, 90, 103, 108-9, 112-15, 119, 124,
    127, 129-30, 132, 137-8, 146, 150
Winchester, Gilbert 122-3
Winney, William 15-19
Wise, Lydia 95
Wolfe, William Francis 16
Woods, Major 134
Worman, Ellen 95
Worthington, Dr 124
Wyatt, Mr 59-60

York 15-19
Young, John 40-1
Young, PC 45

Other titles published by The History Press

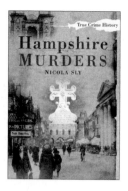

Hampshire Murders
NICOLA SLY

Life in the historic county of Hampshire has not always been peaceful, for over the years it has experienced numerous murders. These include the killing of 'Sweet Fanny Adams' in 1867 and the gun battle in the village of Kingsclere in 1944, which resulted in the deaths of three people. Nicola Sly's carefully researched, well-illustrated and enthralling text will appeal to anyone interested in the shady side of Hampshire's history, and should give much food for thought.

978 0 7509 5106 7

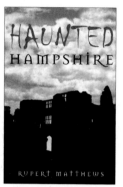

Haunted Hampshire
RUPERT MATTHEWS

The ghosts and phantoms of Hampshire are no less varied than the landscape that they inhabit. There are spectres of the rich and famous to be encountered – Florence Nightingale and King William II among them – but there are also the wraiths of penniless peddlers and struggling workmen to be met. From tales of ghosts inhabiting theatres, pubs and lanes to personal experiences of sightings, this book is guaranteed to thrill and scare, and will be of interest to anyone keen to learn more about one of the country's most haunted areas.

978 0 7524 4862 6

Hanged at Winchester
STEVE FIELDING

Until hanging was abolished in the 1960s Winchester Prison was the main centre of execution for those convicted of murder both in Hampshire and its neighbouring counties. Among the executions carried out here was that of soldier Abraham Goldenberg, hanged for the murder of a bank clerk; William Podmore, convicted in 1930 of killing a garage owner in Southampton; and two Polish refugees who murdered a have-a-go hero during a bungled bank robbery. Steve Fielding's highly readable new book features each of the twenty-nine cases in one volume for the first time and is fully illustrated with photographs, news cuttings, rare documents and drawings.

978 0 7524 5707 9

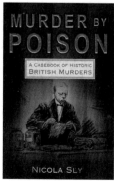

Murder by Poison: A Casebook of Historic British Murders
NICOLA SLY

Readily obtainable and almost undetectable prior to advances in forensic science during the twentieth century, poison was considered the ideal method of murder and many of its exponents failed to stop at just one victim. Along with the most notorious cases of murder by poison in the country – such as those of Mary Ann Cotton and Dr Thomas Neil Cream – this book also features many of the cases that did not make national headlines, examining not only the methods and motives but also the real stories of the perpetrators and their victims.

978 0 7524 5065 0

Visit our website and discover thousands of other History Press books.

www.thehistorypress.co.uk